Aztlán: Origin and Ethnology

In memory of my youngest daughter, Xochitl

Xochitl continues to live in us and like a flower reminds us to appreciate the beauty of life.

Copyright 2016© by Alfredo Acosta Figueroa
Cuna de Aztlán, Blythe, California

First Printing 2017

Other Publications by the Author
Ancient Footprints of the Colorado River, 2013

All Rights Reserved

Published by La Cuna de Aztlán Publishing Company

Front Cover: Aubin Codex

No part of this work may be reproduced or transmitted in any form or by any means, electronic or mechanical, including photocopying, recording or by any information storage and retrieval system without written permission from the author, except for the inclusion of brief quotations in a review.

ISBN 978-0-9962147-5-9

Omeyocan Diamond
Place of the Two Hearts

Ancient Footprints of the Colorado River

Ometéotl

Omeyocan Place of the Two Hearts

For the Indigenous people, since time immemorial every physical being has its cosmic spiritual duality. The Blythe Giant Intaglios are the focal point of the creation. When looking at the Blythe Intaglios, there are three humanoid images. The male image (geoglyph) is Ometecuhtli, Ome means two, the physical and the spiritual. Tecuhtli means male. The female is Omecihuatl, ome, again means the physical and spiritual. Cihuatl means female. The third humanoid image represents the Creator, Ometeotl. In this case Ome means the spirituality of the male and female. Teotl means energy, the Creator. Ometeotl is the supreme metaphysical being of all things.

Contents

Acknowledgements 1
Special Recognition/Advertance 3
Foreword...4
Preface...6
Introduction 7
Aztlán, Place of Origin of the
Azteca/Mexica on the Colorado River.......8
The Meaning of Aztlán.........................10
Coatepetl-Center of the World-
Axis Mundi 13
Big Maria Mountain Range..................14
Historians and Codices.......................16
The Blythe Giant Intaglios.................. 22
Moon Mountain Twin Peaks.................26
In Search of Aztlán.............................35
The Destruction of the Island of Aztlán....38
Aztlán: Consciousness in the Southwest....40
Orgullo de Aztlán-Pride of Aztlán..........41
Mexico/Aztlán on the Colorado River
And Its Relationship
to Mexico/Tenochtitlan........................42
Chimalma 48
Nuhu (The People)..............................54
The Bird Songs-Oral History of the
Migrations From Aztlán 58
Why wasn't Aztlán Revealed Before?........63
Codex Telleriano Remensis Erroneous
Mathematical Measurement of time 66
52-year Cycle Mathematical
Breakdown...67
Florencio Yescas 74
Cuauhtémoc's Spiritual March 76
Conclusion...80
Why don't we know the truth in
the United States?...............................81
Tres Cientificos 82
What is going to happen after 2012?...........83
Biography of Alfredo Acosta Figueroa.....86
Nahuatl/Mexica Glossary 91
Bibliography......................................96

Illustrations

1. Aubin Codex, Aztlán
2. Blue Heron, Symbol of Aztlán
3. Tovar Codex, Fold 89
4. Big Maria Mountain Range
5. Map-Lower Colorado River Basin Valleys
6. Map-Indigenous Reservations, Lower Colorado River Valleys
7. Google Earth Map, Blythe Giant Intaglios
8. Zoomed Google Earth Map
9. 1881 Map
10. Ometeotl, Blythe Giant Intaglios
11. Vaticanus A Codex, First Sun
12. The Moon Mountains
13. Twin Peaks Moon Mts. with the sun rising
14. Vindobonensis Codex, Fold 23
15. Sun Impregnating Mother Earth Petroglyph
16. Xicomoztoc-Place of Birthing of Humans
17. Comparison of the petroglyph with the Historia Tolteca-Chichimeca Codex
18. Azcatitlan Codex, Fold 5, Xicomoztoc, the birthing of humans.
19. Big Maria Mountain in the afternoon during winter solstice.
20. Images of the Meaning of Mexico
21. The Tlaltecuhtli Idol
22. The rabbit on the moon- Mexica Codex
23. White Limestone Eagle Image-Mixcoatlcuauhtli
24. Fundacion de Mexico/Tenochtitlan
25. Aztlan-Land of the Whiteness
26. Panoramic view of the Whiteness of the Big Maria Mts.
27. What remains of the Island of Aztlán
28. The First Sunrise, Beginning of the First Sun-Vindobonensis Codex Fold 23
29. 1847 Treaty of Guadalupe Hidalgo Map
30. Zoomed Treaty of Guadalupe Hidalgo Map on the Colorado River
31. Chimalma's Face Image on the Big Maria Mts.
32. Chimalma with her shield as one of the four Teomamas, Boturini Codex, Fold 3
33. Chimalma (left) with her shield and Quetzalcoatl, Boturini Codex, Fold 1
34. Chimalma's Idol image in the Mayan culture
35. Chimalma Shield pictograph at Painted Rock, Texas
36. Big Maria Mt. Range
37. Zoomed Big Maria Mountains
38. Four Peaks of the Big Maria Mts.
39. Vindobonensis Codex, Fold 52 Prelude in the Sky
40. The Birthing/ Ending of Nuhu (The People)
41. Nuhu
42. North end, east side of McCoy Mts.
43. Nuhu on north end, east side of McCoy Mts.
44. Siguenza Codex, Migration from Aztlan
45. Codice Mexicanus, Lamina XVIII
46. Huehuetlapallan on the Colorado River
47. Migrations to the four directions centered in the Palo Verde/Parker Valleys
48. Boturini Codex, Fold 1 and 2
49. Telleriano Remensis Codex
50. Five Suns of the Era of Pisces

51. Pleiades: The Seven Sisters Constellation
52. Petroglyph of the Pleiades Star Cluster
53. Pleiades Star Cluster Geoglyph Images at Blythe Giant Intaglios
54. 52-year cycle- Day Lunar and Solar Calendars
55. Huitzilopochtli and its relation to the Mexica New Fire Ceremony
56. New Fire Ceremony at Cerro Estrella in Mexico City, Mexico
57. New Fire Ceremony- Florentine Codex
58. Broken pottery found at base of the Mule Mts.
59. Florencio Yescas
60. Cuauhtemoc's Spiritual March, Return to Aztlan
61. The Cuauhtémoc Spiritual Pilgrimage at the Tribal Administration
62. Why we don't know the truth in the United States.
63. Re-encounter with our spiritual, cultural and ancestral roots
64. Alfredo Acosta Figueroa, the author

Acknowledgements

This book was made possible thanks to the arduous work of the following people. We are indebted to them for their generous dedication and contribution in this monumental task.

We will forever be grateful to my daughters, Maria "Machi" Rivera for financing this project and Demesia Patricia Robles, who for the past two decades has been in the forefront of editing and composing our research. We are also very thankful to Juan Ulloa, Jorge Hernandez and Enrique Ramirez whom have always been in full support of our endeavors in seeking the roots of the truth.

We would like to give Cesar Guevara a special recognition for arranging and designing the chapters and illustrations in our book. We are thankful to Cecilia Navarro for typing the draft arrangement of the book.

Our appreciation to Mr. Boma Johnson, a retired Bureau of Land Management archeologist, for his invaluable assistance, contribution and foresight in identifying the location of many geoglyphs and sacred sites located along the Colorado River extending from Needles, California, in the north down to Yuma, Arizona, in the south. These geoglyphs are some of the archaeological missing links to the location of the long-sought 'mystical' Aztlán.

We are very fortunate that Indigenous traditionalists have survived the past 500 years of European onslaught. Without the Indigenous persistence in conserving the cosmic archetype traditional culture, it would have been very difficult to present this evidence. Special recognition goes to the invaluable information provided by the Mojave Elders, Ron Van Fleet Sr., Steve Lopez and Llewelyn Barrackman (deceased) and our Chemehuevi Elders, Phil Smith, Ignacio "Nacho" Macias, Henry Ortiz Sr.(deceased), Luis Solaiza (deceased), Pablo Solaiza (deceased) and Gilbert Lopez Leivas (deceased).

We are very thankful to the following people for providing us with their knowledge of the Mexica/Mayan culture. They were instrumental in assisting us with the interpretation of the Mexica/Mayan codices, and other information concerning our traditional cosmic Indigenous culture. We would like to acknowledge Professor Jose Manuel Garcia "Acamapixtli," Nahuatlaca/Lecturer of the Mexica Tradition and writer, Maestra Estrella Newman (now deceased), one of the promoters of the Mexicanidad Movement and confidant of the 12th descendent of Cuauhtemoc, Dr. Salvador Rodriguez (deceased) and to Hunbatz-Men, Mayan Shaman and traditionalist (deceased). We have been empowered by our nihilistic attitude towards European dominance.

We are grateful to Patricia Amblin who produced the video "The Five Suns". We correlated many codices with the local geoglyphs, mountain images, petroglyphs, solstice, equinoxes and other sacred sites that lie in the surrounding Colorado River Valleys. "The Five Suns" video facilitated the relationship with the above mentioned sacred sites and local Mojave and Chemehuevi history.

Above all, we are forever indebted to the Creator for bestowing upon us the knowledge to seek our cosmic cultural traditional roots.

Special Recognition

One day in 1958, Francisco Figueroa, my father's cousin, a professor in Nogales and Trincheras, Sonora gave my brother Miguel "Mike" Figueroa, a book, *Nociones de Historia de Sonora* by Laureano Calvo Berber. He told Mike to give it to me because the book identified most of the tribes that migrated south to Mexico came from Aztlán which is situated in the confluences of the Colorado and Gila Rivers. He said that I was on the right track in seeking the location of Aztlán in the Colorado River Valley.

The book indicates that the Toltecas are regarded as one of the first to leave from Huehuetlapallan and began their migration on the Gila River where they made one of their first settlements, Casa Grande on the Gila River. From the Gila River, they continued south and settled in Trincheras, Sonora. On the migration, the Cahitas (Yaquis & Mayos) branched off the Toltecas and settled at the area of El Rio Yaqui, Sonora.

The Athapaskans in Alaska have in their oral history tradition that they came from the Colorado and Gila Rivers junction, two ice ages ago. (Chief Gary Harrison)

This is one of the major sources that gives credence to the location of Aztlán and motivated me to pursue its origin in a more devout effort.

Advertance

"It is very important that the persons who want to know the Mexica way of thinking have to understand the meaning of the Nahualismo of the Creator's images and humans."

Ignacio Bernal, Tenochtitlan, En Una Isla 1984

The Nahualismo is the spiritual belief that the individual's life is unified with an animal image and that animal image is the Nahualli of that person. The animal is the Nahualli of the Creator in all its images. It is called Ipalnemohuani, " He who no name yet has all the names."

The Natives of the American continent (Anahuac) never disassociated themselves from the cosmic cultural archetype. Every season, month, day, hour and minute has its cosmic counterpart of the truth of our existence on earth.

Foreword

For the past century, Aztlán has been an idea, a state of mind that has empowered and inspired millions of Chicanos to action benefiting themselves and the world around them. That it was also very likely the name of a physical parcel of land somewhere in the southwestern U.S. has been overridden by the mystical aura conveyed in the very name from the first days it began to circulate among activist Chicanos.

That Alfredo Figueroa has pinpointed its location within a few square-miles' area of California is a remarkable achievement. For generations, its location was hinted at by scholars and indigenous peoples but only one man that I know of has had the patience and drive to pursue his dream of finding the source. Alfredo Figueroa has been telling everyone for at least a couple of decades that the "cuna de Aztlán lay not far from his home.

Credit for unveiling the concept of Aztlán as a touchstone for the Chicano Movement goes to Alurista (Alberto Urista), a poet whose writings in themselves are seminal to the evolution of the Chicano Movement as a blending of art with the quest for social justice. It's not a coincidence from my point of view that Aztlán, a word bridging thousands of years and many cultures, was resurrected by a poet, a maker of words. The idea of Aztlán as the original home of the people who founded the Azteca Empire and what is now Mexico transformed into part of the mystique which undergirded the socio-political impulse behind the Chicano Movement of the late 1960s to early 1970s.

The home of the people who eventually occupied what is now Mexico City and built a vast empire had been hinted at by noted historians. William H. Prescott in his History of the Conquest of Mexico (1843) and Alvin
M. Josephy, Jr., in The Indian Heritage (1968) allude to Aztlán's original site somewhere in the southwestern U.S. In Mexico, a Traves de los Siglos (1939), a compendium of Mexican historians' research, the editors remark on the artifacts and human settlements in various southwestern states that point to where their ancestors dwelled before they began "the pilgrimage to found Teotihuacan.

To the native peoples of the Colorado River Indian Tribes, the site was always known. "Though the Natives of the Colorado Indian Tribes knew its origin," Figueroa states, "it had never been publicized until now. The Island of Aztlán, he state is approximately 20 miles northeast of Blythe, California, on the Colorado River Indian Tribes Reservation in an area called Palo Verde/Parker Valley."

So in a way the location of Aztlán has been an open secret. Everybody knew where the Aztecas came from. No one, until Figueroa, had done the hard work to pinpoint it. As he says, "This is the place of the ancestors of millions of today's Indigenous people. Although it has been sought for centuries, Aztlán's whereabouts until now, was a mystery.

I think this distinction is what drove Figueroa to persist in his search. He says, "In the hearts and minds of Xicanos, the location of their ancestral homeland, Aztlán was just a mystery, not a myth." He held to that thought, that Aztlán had truly existed, that it had not been just a fanciful piece of folklore.

 Figueroa has cleared away the mystery and identified the ancestral home of the Azteca/Mexica and the conceptual birthplace of us Chicano Indios. However, two questions come to mind:

 Will professional archaeologists and lettered historians challenge Figueroa's findings? Other researchers, bent on discrediting his findings, may follow the trail that Figueroa has laid out, re-examine the intaglios that are reflected in later Mexican artifacts, re-analyze the codices which literally point the way with footprints inked onto parchment linking the two worlds, and sift over again the testimony of indigenous peoples over hundreds of years? The debate may not be over.

 Has the mystery or mystique been ripped away? Do we see clearly now and therefore no longer wonder?

 To me, this is the most intriguing question of any that might be put. Since the concept of Aztlán first appeared in a Chicano setting, in the Plan de Aztlán, issued on March 31, 1969, in Denver, Colorado, it has represented far more than a mystery or a vague site on a map, because ultimately the place we call Aztlán resides within us, Chicanos. In Chicano Manifesto (1971, 1996), which I wrote over a two-year period before it was published in the 1971, I stated:

 "My people have come in fulfillment of a cosmic cycle from ancient Aztlán, the seed ground of the great civilization of Anahuac to <u>modern Aztlán</u>... We have rediscovered Aztlán in ourselves."

 So while Figueroa has resolved a question that has hung in the air for decades, where the founders of Aztlán had actually lived, the debate may still continue and intensify. So be it: the more discussion, the greater attention and understanding within the Chicano community.

 For not matter where Aztlán is physically, its relevance to us Chicanos as a conceptual foundation for an ever-evolving worldview--many of us call it, Chicanismo--is its transcendental value.

Armando Rendón

La Bahía de San Francisco

February 10, 2015

Preface

The Ancient four-thousand-year-old City of Troy and the Trojan Wars were considered myths until the German Archaeologist Heinrich Schielmann found Troy by studying the ancient legends and maps of Troy.

Likewise, Alfredo Acosta Figueroa has located the site of origin of the Aztecs, long considered by many to be a myth. The site of Aztlan/Land of the Herons/the Land of Origin of the Aztecs has been found. It has never been completely hidden. Mr. Figueroa has spent about sixty years studying this. By careful study of the Giant Geoglyphs, the Mountains and the Images that they clearly contain and comparing them to the Aztec Codices and Monuments in Mexico he shows how the image clearly reflect their legends of their beloved site of origin, Aztlan. He also has studied the place names in Spanish, English and several Native American Languages in reaching his conclusions. Old maps such as the Treaty of Guadalupe Hidalgo illustrated in his book clearly show that the Blythe, California area is the Cradle of Aztlan, the place of origin of the Aztecs. They also show the early migration route taken by the Aztecs on their migration to Tenochtitlan (Mexico City).

I have visited the Geoglyphs with Alfredo Figueroa several times and have seen the reflections of the images of Aztec Cosmology in the Mountains surrounding Blythe. I am convinced without a doubt that he is correct and that this knowledge need to be revealed to the World

Dr. Arthur Cushman

Introduction

Aztlán is the mystical place of origin of the Mexica people. It is beyond a mere physical location. Aztlán has become a metaphoric, geographic, historical and spiritual home to millions of Indigenous people of North America.

Aztlán was in fact mystical and not mythical as portrayed by the established mainstream teachings. Historians and investigators were always looking for Aztlán in Mesoamerica. Aztlán remained elusive primarily due to lack of scientific cross-reference study of the Mexica codex, artifacts and sacred ruins from Mexico with the lower Colorado River Basin intaglios, geoglyphs, petroglyphs, pictographs, mountain images, equinoxes, solstices, local Native songs, language and folklore.

The original Indigenous people were called Azteca and they built dikes to contain the lake where the Island of Aztlán was, located on the Colorado River Indian Tribes Reservation. The Mojave called the lake, Whalia Hanyo (Moon Lake) and Metzliapan is what the Azteca called it in Nahuatl.

During the height of the Xicano Movement in the 1960s-70s, once again the word, Aztlán resurged. Aztlán was not thought of as a mythical place but as a long lost mystical Aztlán. In their hearts, Xicanos were longing to now where Aztlán was and knew that it was to be found in the Southwest United States. This is why "Viva Aztlán" became the rallying cry that motivated them to continue seeking the roots of the truth of their origin.

Aztlán
Place of Origin of the Azteca/Mexica on the Colorado River

The Mexica believed Aztlán was the earthly paradise where their ancestors lived. Aztlán's location has always been debated by historians. According to the ancient legend of the Mexica codices, the Mexica place of origin was called Aztlán, Xicomoztoc, Tamoanchan, Coatepetl and Huehuetlapallan. It was located somewhere in Northwest Mexico or Southwest United States.

Aztlán is the place most commonly referred to as the place of origin of the Azteca/Mexica. This is the place of the ancestor of millions of today's Indigenous people. Although it has been sought for centuries, Aztlán's whereabouts until now, was a mystery. Though the Natives of the Colorado River knew its origin, it has never been publicized until now. The Island of Aztlán was approximately 20 miles northeast of Blythe, California in the Parker Valley It was at the base of the Moon Mountains on the Colorado River Indian Tribes Reservation across from the Blythe Giant Intaglios, surrounded by Lake Mexico.

Ill 1

Island of Aztlán from the Aubin Codex

For centuries, the location of Aztlán had not been revealed because there had not been a modern-day study of the Lower Colorado River Basin Valleys within the confluence of the Colorado and Gila Rivers and because it was not the policy of the traditional Natives to reveal sacred sites due to fear of the sites being destroyed by the overall population and the government policies.

The Island of Aztlán was destroyed by the annual floods of the Colorado River that eventually destroyed all the ancient Aztec structures leaving only the ruins of the vestige of some of the foundations. This was before the current levees and dams were built. Those ruins are part of the evidence of the location of the Island of Aztlán and the old dried saline river bed lake channel that formed a slough at the base of the Moon Mountain was part of Lake Mexico. These are the only physical remains of the lake and the Island of Aztlán. (Gilbert Leivas, Mike Martinez)

Aztlán was not just the place of origin for the Azteca but for all the Native people of Cemanahuac (North American Continent) and Tawantinsuyu (South American Continent). When the Azteca left to the four directions on their migrations, they would name certain sites in honor of the different images of the Creator that they left behind in the Lower Colorado River Valleys.

They were never doubtful of their place in history. Every day was guided by a cosmic event.

Well-known historian, Paul Kirchhoff coined the phrase, "Mesoamerica" and now we have Aridamerica and Oasisamerica, the super regions. With most of the interest in research of Aztlán focused in Mesoamerica, it is no wonder the location of Aztlán has not been identified in modern day. An in-depth study has never been done on the Lower Colorado River Basin and its connection to the people in Mexico and Aztlán. The super regions cannot be seen as independent regions. They must be considered as a whole if we are to comprehend the diversity and the reality of the Nahua/Mexica traditions and their origins.

The geographical location of Mexico/Aztlán is herein identified as the area of the Palo Verde/Parker Valleys on the lower Colorado River that borders the current states of Arizona and California. The ancient Indigenous nations, Azteca/Mexica left from Mexico/Aztlán on the Colorado River to settle in Mexico/Tenochtitlan.

Thanks to the ancient footprints of the Colorado River left by our ancestors that escaped total destruction over the past 500 years of the European invasion, we have been able to put this research together. These footprints are evidence to the truth of the origin of our ancestors, the Azteca/Mexica. With the cross-reference studies of our findings on the Colorado River and its surroundings and the few Mexica codices that also escaped European destruction, we were able to identify where the true location of Aztlán is. This intensive investigation and historical account seeks to answer the three main anthropological questions asked by anthropologists and archaeologists, "Where did we come from?" "Why are we here?" and "Where did we come?"

The Meaning of Aztlán

Aztlán has many meanings but the most recognized and accepted has been "The place of the heron" based on the abundance of herons in the Palo Verde/Parker Valleys.

Ill 2

Blue Heron, Symbol of Aztlán
(Photo by Wes Martin, Cibola Wildlife Refuge)

Aztatl relates to the Heron/Ciguenza and comes from the word Aztlán. It is the most popular term and symbol used especially by the Mexica/Xicano(a). Every autumn many herons, cranes, ducks, egrets and many more species migrate south from Canada to Mexico. On their way to Mexico, they follow the Lower Colorado River to its delta at the Gulf of California. Although some herons live year-round in the Palo Verde/Parker Valleys, many of them and other fowl from the north stay all winter along the river in the wildlife refuges such as Havasu, Cibola or Imperial. Others, however, seek shelter in the Lower Colorado River delta in the Mexicali Valley or in the Salton Sea area. (Cibola National Wildlife Bulletin).

Aztlán is derived from Aztl-Aztli-Wing, Lan-Place, place of the wing. It is referred as the eagle's wing because of the big white limestone eagle with its wings spread out on the Big Maria Mountain overlooking the Palo Verde Valley.

Aztapiltic, Land of the Whiteness refers to Aztlán. In the Big Maria and Little Maria Mountains are large white limestone images that are seen on the mountainside in the Palo Verde/Parker Valleys. The main white limestone image is the large white limestone eagle that has a wingspread of over 1/2 mile and is seen from West Blythe (Acacitli). Northwest of the eagle image on the mountainside are the two white limestone snake images and many other images on the side of the mountain. The big snake-like images are seen parallel to the mountain crest.

Azcalli, another important word that relates to Aztlán, is alabaster, a whitish variety of gypsum. Alabaster in Nahuatl is Tiza meaning chalk. The Little Maria and Big Maria Mountains are where the U.S. Gypsum Company mined gypsum and made wallboard for 50 years in Midland, Ca, 23 miles northwest of Blythe. On the eastern part of the Riverside Mountains is another large gypsum deposit. In the codices, the Riverside Mountains represent the Milky Way (Mixcoatl) meaning cloud of serpents. In the Mojave language, the Riverside Mountains are called Avi-Vatay (the long house). The large gypsum deposit reaches the west bank of the Colorado River.

In the book, "Memorial Breve Acerca de la Fundacion de La Ciudad de Colhuacan" by Domingo Francisco de San Anton Munon Chimalphin Cuauhtlehuanitzin, he mentions Tizapan meaning Tiza (gypsum), apan (by the water), gypsum by the water. In the story "Topiltzin Acatl," Quetzalcoatl departs from Tizapan to Tlapallan (east) where he is called by the rising sun and he becomes the morning star (Venus). The wise ancient people said, "He lives yet. He has not died and will come again to rule." On the first fold of the Aubin codex is Huemac (Big Hand) on top of the Island of Aztlán looking east.

Tonallatlatzaliztli, "Land of the Rising Sun" is another meaning. The sun rising during the equinoxes between Moon Mountain twin peaks when seen from the Blythe Giant Intaglios forms the appearance of a "U" in the Moon Mountains (east above the location of the Island of Aztlán) located on the Colorado River Indian Tribes Reservation. Aztlán refers to Tonallatlatzcaliztli, the original meaning of the "Great Sun", the "Calm". This sun rising is the beginning of the First Sun of the Five Suns on the Aztec Sunstone calendar.

The Twin Peaks represent the vulva of Mother Earth, Tonantzin. This represents Mother Earth being impregnated by Father Sun. This image is shown in the Vindobonensis Codex, Fold 52.

After Mother Earth is impregnated during the morning twilight hour, the sun rays shine on the ridge of the Big Maria Mountain Range. The first image is the pyramid-like image called Tonatiuhichan, the house of the Sun and immediately on the human face of Huitzilopochtli (facing south) and on the head of Cihuatcoatl peak facing north toward Topock Maze (Mictlan).

The Island of Aztlán was just below the twin peaks in the Parker Valley. The lake surrounding the island was Metzliapan (Moon Lake) and it was formed by the meandering Colorado River thousands

of years ago.

The original Indigenous people called Azteca built dikes to contain the lake. After the Mexica migrated from Aztlán, the Hokan linguistic family moved in. The Mojave called the lake, Whalia Hanyo (Moon Lake). This same name was carried down to present day Mexico City where the lake was also called Metzliapan and the island was named Tenochtitlan.

Azteca is derived from Aztlán. Azteca is plural and Aztlánteca is singular. The Azteca were the first people. The Boturini Codex, fold 5 shows the glyph of the breaking tree (Tamoanchan). It has the Creator, Mecitli, in the image of Huitzilopochtli (hummingbird) telling the Azteca to change their name to Mexica in honor of him, the Creator's image, who descended from the cosmos.

Mecitli is deciphered as: Me (Mecitli)-moon, Citli-jackrabbit; overall Mecitli means jackrabbit on the moon. In other words, the Mexica are named after Mexitli (Mecitli), jackrabbit on the moon.

The most recent cosmic event of the breaking of the tree (Tamoanchan/Granite Peak) was on May 15, 2002 when the Gemini twins in line with the five-planet alignment descended on Granite Peak at approximately 12 midnight. Granite Peak is 45 miles northwest of Acacitli (West Blythe) and it looks like a large pyramid at the northwest end of the McCoy Valley.

The jackrabbit image (Mecitli) on the crescent moon is formed by Jupiter's position in the middle of the Gemini twins, Pollux and Castor. Jupiter forms the nose of the jackrabbit face and his long ears extend to the stars of Pollux and Castor. The jackrabbit is sitting on its hind legs that are part of the lower Gemini image in the cosmos. During the alignment of the planets, the crescent moon is to the right of Jupiter. This is the metamorphosing of the jackrabbit on the moon. That is why the jackrabbit is manifested on the moon similar to the glyph that is on a Mayan vessel in the American Museum of Natural History in New York City.

When Gemini descends on Granite Peak, the letter "C" converts into the letter "X" representing the cosmos descending on earth, thus we have the name of Mexica. Both Azteca and Mexica names are appropriate for the Indigenous that came from the Colorado River, Azteca for Aztlán, Mother Earth and Mexica for Father Cosmos.

All these images relate to the Creation story and are inter-related with the Mexica codices.

Coatepetl-Center of the World-Axis Mundi

Ill 3

Tovar Codex, Fold 89 shows Coatepetl (Snake Mountain)

Interpretation of Drawing- The center depicts the mountain of Coatepetl, Big Maria Mountain overlooking West Blythe (Acacitli) on the south. On the mountain is the rattlesnake, Quetzalcoatl snake image facing east. The water image under the mountain is the Colorado River that forms a bend towards the west in the Palo Verde Valley and forms the north mesa. The upper left corner is a banner, Pantli, a house, Calli. a jackrabbit, Citli. Under the jackrabbit is the human sitting on the wicker box which represents the Island of Acacitli. Acacitli was an island where West Blythe is located. The upper right corner is the cactus, Nopal. The cactus is growing from the stone, Tepetl. Under the cactus is the human representing Tenoch sitting on the wicker box that represents the original Island of Tenochtitlan.

The tullies represent Tula, where Huemac ousted Quetzalcoatl. Coatepetl symbolized the center of the axis-mundi. Coatepetl is the first mountain that emerged from the primordial waters, its images all oriented to the four directions of the universe. They correlate to the five different daily shadow images of the sacred sites and the cosmic equinox and solstice events.

Coatepetl's snake images are on the center of the Big Maria mountain range, 10 miles north of Blythe, California where you can see the two large white limestone snake images on the mountainside. One is coming from the east and the other is coming from the west. They meet below the mountain image of Cihuatcoatl (La Llorona).

Big Maria Mountain Range Images

Ill 4

Photo of Big Maria Mountain Range (Coatepetl) taken from West Blythe (Acacitli) is depicted in the Tovar Codex, Fold 90 (Photo by Alfredo A. Figueroa)

Top peak is Crying Woman, La Llorona (3), Cihuatcoatl, pregnant with Huitzilopochtli, looking up and to the east. She has her mouth open because she is crying. Below Cihuatcoatl is the snake with its mouth open facing west (4) ready to eat the goat (2) (at the snake's mouth) facing east. The snake about to gobble the goat depicts the ending of a season. On the left is the snake (1) facing east pursuing a human's head (5), also the end of a season.

The Aztec/Mexica never disassociated themselves from their cosmic archetype cultural tradition. Their entire existence revolved around it and that there was not a single act, public or private that was not tinged by it, even regulated commerce, sports games and war. It intervened in every event in the individual's life from the time he was born until they buried his ashes. It was the basic lesson for the existence of the state itself. (Alfonso Caso)

When the Nahua nations left the Colorado River, they took this knowledge with them. The Olmeca are credited to being the first nation to commemorate the founding of the creation by building pyramids and other structures in Vera Cruz. When the Mexica erected the main temple (Templo Mayor) in Mexico/Tenochtitlan, they did it according to the cosmogonies of their ancestors so they would not forget their place of origin on the Colorado River focused in the Palo Verde/Parker Valleys.

The cosmos-vision of the Mesoamerican communities was reflected by the cultural material like it architecture and its arrangements within the cities. In the center of the sites, they built temples which form decorations and functions would correspond with the cosmic deity dedicated to the image of their cultural ritual framework.

El Templo Mayor in Mexico/Tenochtitlan was inside of a sacred site isolated from the world surrounded by a wall. These temples were constructed to reproduce the Mexica cosmos-vision concept of quincunce, the four directions and center of the world. El Templo Mayor was elevated in the center symbolizing Coatepetl (Snake Mountain), the sacred mountain. It stored the rain, lightning and multitudinous seeds of life.

Situated in the center of the sacred site, El Templo Mayor converted into the Axis Mundi, center of the world for the Mexica. It was the house of the Creator and the place of excellence where the humans would descend to the 9 levels of the inner-world or ascend to the 13 levels in the cosmos. It was the place where the humans went to make offerings and petitions to the Creator. (Arqueologia Mexican Magazine, Vol XVI NO 91 May/June 2008)

Historians and Codices

Most historians who have written about Aztlán speculate that the Nahua came from Northwest Mexico or Southwest United States. However, modern day researchers and archaeologists have not been able to link the Azteca/Mexica with their ancient homeland of Aztlán, giving rise to the misconception that Aztlán existed only in myth. Historians base their concepts on the old theory of the Hohokam (People who have gone) or the Anazasi (Ancient People). They don't know where they went to.

One of the main centers of the Hohokam was Sacaton, Arizona, on the Gila River near Casa Grande National Monument. From there, they went south, finally settling in the area of Zacatecas, Sacaton broken down is Saca-zacate-grass, ton-big; place of the big grass. Zacatecas is place of the grass. The Hohokam from Sacaton finally settled in Zacatecas and close to the capitol is the town of Zacaton.

Aztlán is clearly depicted in the Mexica Codices such as the Boturini, Aubin, Siguenza and Mexicanus. The Siguenza and Mexicanus have a bird telling the people "Tihui, Tihui" (go forward and find your house). The bird in the form of the hummingbird and eagle is the bird that leads the Uto-Aztecan people from Aztlán on the Colorado River and leads the Hokan Linguistic families (Mojave, Quechan, Cocopah, etc.) up to the Colorado River. The popular "Bird Songs" relate to the bird leading the people and is one of the oldest chants on the North American continent.

The Aubin Codex shows Aztlán as an island and a hill (Tepetl) with a human image (Huemac, big hand) standing at the top of it. On each side of the hill are 2 glyphs, representing a house (Calli). A Spanish interpreter of the codex added the word "Azteca" on top of the house images and at the bottom of the hill he wrote "Aztlán".

Chilmalpahin Cuaugtlehuanitin, native of Chalco-Amaguemecan (near present day Mexico City) and descendant of the Tlatoani of Tenochtitlan, places Aztlán in California, in the vast region surrounding the confluence of the Colorado and Gila Rivers. He says it is from the region that the Nahua/Azteca migrated south during several different eras, and there is newer archaeological, linguistic and ethnological research to support his conclusions.

Dr. Cecilio Robledo's 1990 "Diccionario de Mitologia Nahuatl" claims that Aztlán is a place originally occupied by "Los Mexicanos," a name that was derived from the name Azteca. He writes that Aztlán is generally believed to have been north of the Gulf of California and adds that there is a linguistic theory correlating the Nahuatl language (spoken by the Azteca) with that spoken by Natives in Arizona. Most social scientists place Aztlán in the north of Mexico, in what is now the Southwest United States. Robledo concludes that the Azteca went south from there on their migration.

In his journal, "El Ombligo de la Luna, " Dr. Alfonso Caso says that Mexico means "in the center of the moon," or "in the center of the lake of the moon," In Nahuatl, it is "Metzliapan." Dr. Caso goes on to say that Mexico and Tenochtitlan, the island (modern day Mexico City), were named like that because "it reminded the Nahua nations of their ancient place of origin of Aztlán, the place the Gods ordered them to leave.

These two interpretations by Caso and Robledo are the two most quoted by historical research and chronicles.

The historians have overlooked the truth of the oral traditional history of the Indigenous Elders of the Lower Colorado River Basin. They have not pursued the connection of the Indigenous people along the Colorado River to the Native Nations from Mexico that left the Colorado River at different intervals. The Indigenous people left to the four directions. Some Nations went south and some went east through the Hopi and Navajo lands. The Athapaskans went north to Alaska.

In the hearts and minds of Xicanos, the location of their ancestral homeland, Aztlán was just a mystery, not a myth but to the Natives of the Colorado River Indian Tribes, the site was always known.

Ancient Footprints of the Colorado River
Sacred Geoglyph Sites

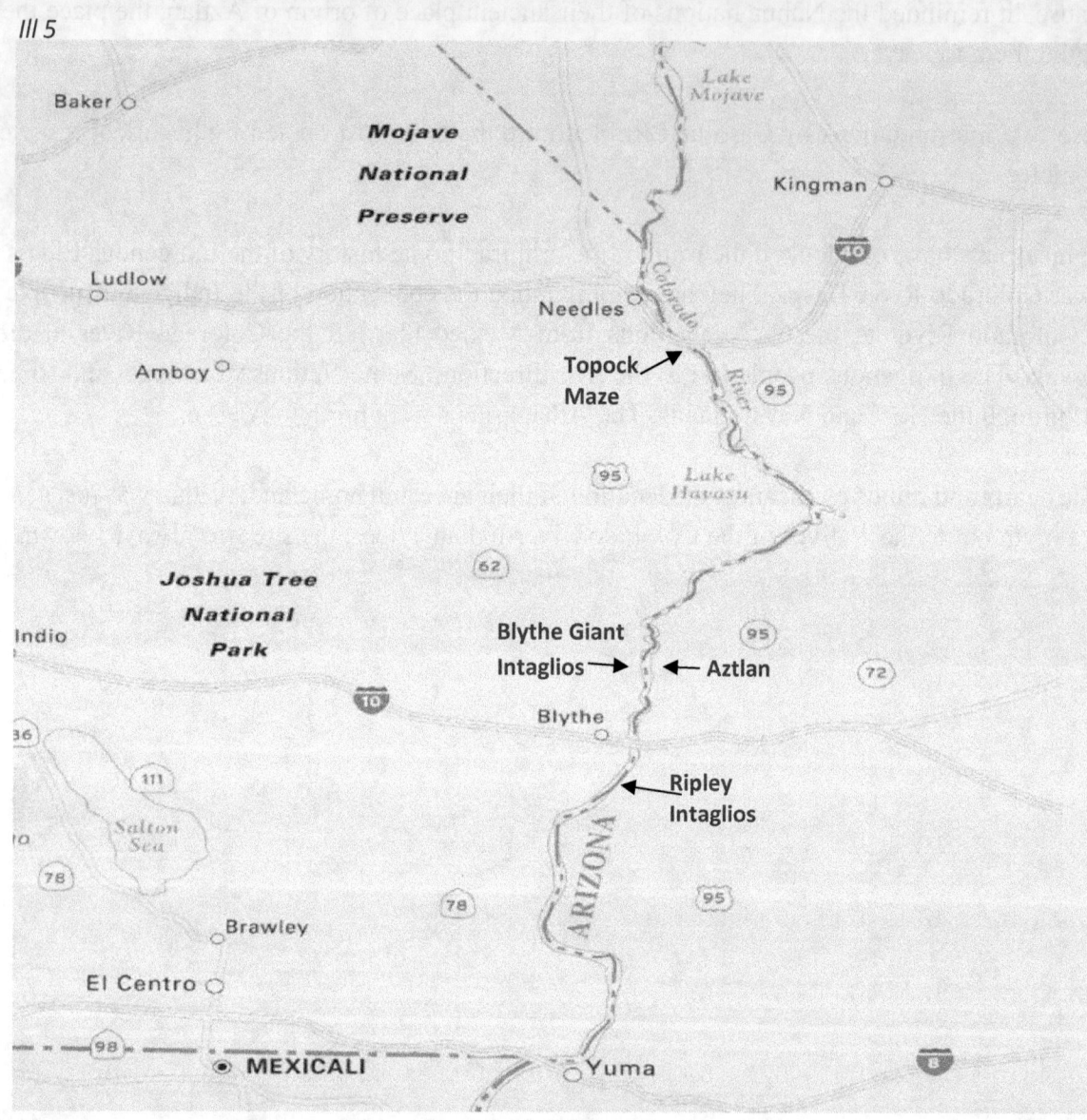

Map of the Lower Colorado River Basin Valleys that identifies some of the sacred geoglyphs that relate to the Creation Story and the location of the Island of Aztlán where the Mexica migrated to the four directions. (Sacred sites and Intaglios included by Alfredo A. Figueroa)

Map of Indigenous Reservations on the Lower Colorado River Valleys

Ill 6

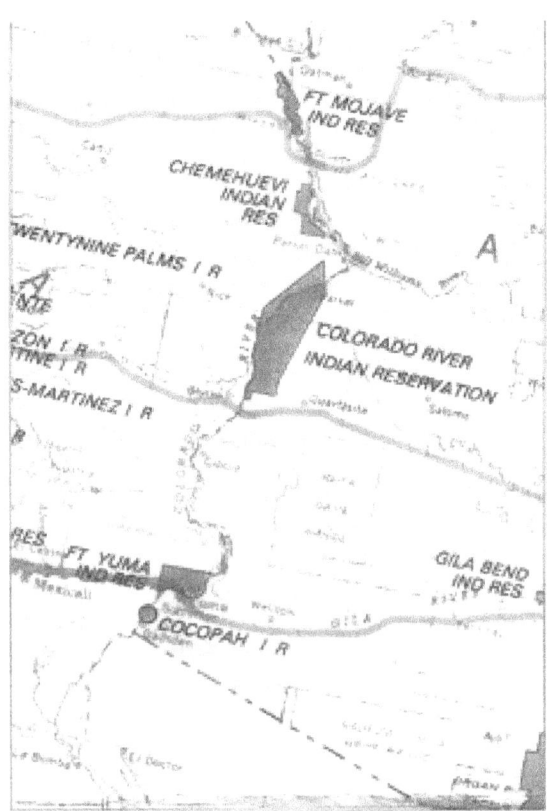

The lower Colorado River Basin has been the home of many Indigenous linguistic families which at one time or another left to the four directions and returned. Some of those nations have come full circle returning to the Colorado River.

Their migration is symbolized by the Four Movements, in Nahuatl called Nahui-Ollin. Some of the nations settled permanently in the area and other such as the Athapaskans left the Colorado River and went north to Alaska before the last Ice Age according to Chief Gary Harrison of the Athapaskan tribe. Other nations such as the Azteca and Olmeca went south thousands of years ago. The Chichimeca followed afterwards, then the Tolteca, Yaqui and finally the Mexica in approximately 1067 A.D. There are five Native Reservations in the lower Colorado River Basin Valleys including Fort Mojave near Needles, California in the north, Chemehuevi, Colorado River Indian Tribes, Quechan and Cocopah, south of Yuma. Of these five, the Mojave and Chemehuevi are most prominent in the Palo Verde/Parker Valleys.

Each Native Tribe has a unique identity and interpretation of the creation story given to them by the Creator. Yet, all the tribes relate to a similar cosmic tradition of the Creator. The oral cosmic cultural traditional knowledge is still alive despite years of the policy, "Kill the Indian, Save the Man" by the United States Government.

Google Earth Map of Blythe Giant Intaglios and the Location of the Island of Aztlán

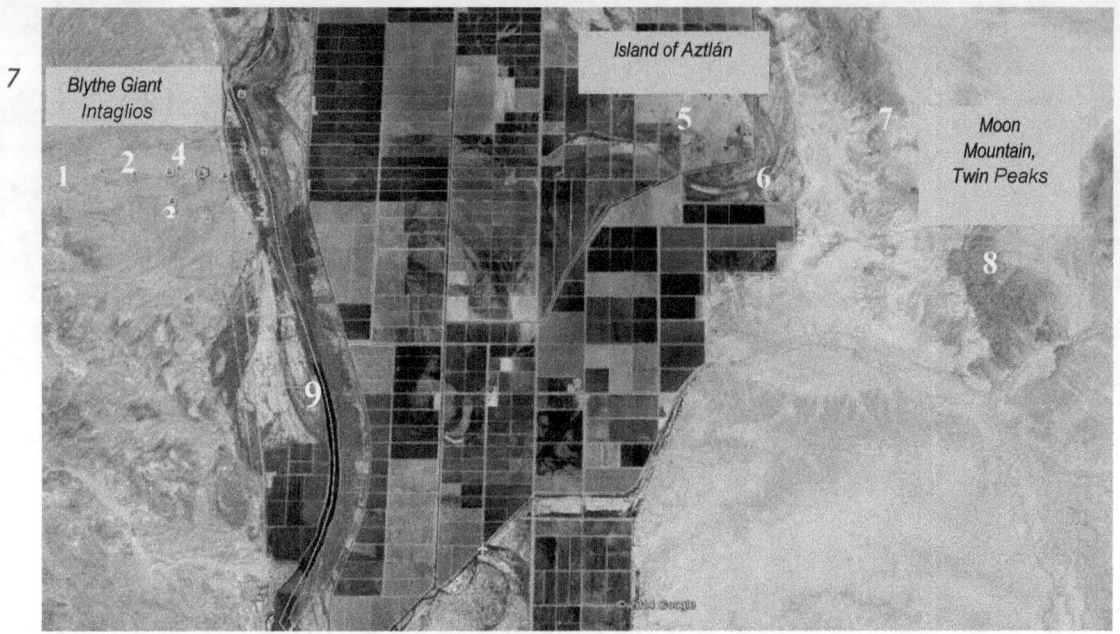

1. Altar (small hill) overlooking Blythe Giant Intaglios, 2. Ometeotl, the Creator, 3. Omecihuatl, the woman, 4. Ometecuhtli, the man, 5. Island of Aztlán, 6. Old Lake Mexico Slough, 7. Twin North Peak, 8. Twin South Peak, 9. Colorado River

Zoomed Google Earth Map shows the Island of Aztlán and Metzliapan (Old Lake Mexico) Slough.

1881 Arizona Map

Ill 9

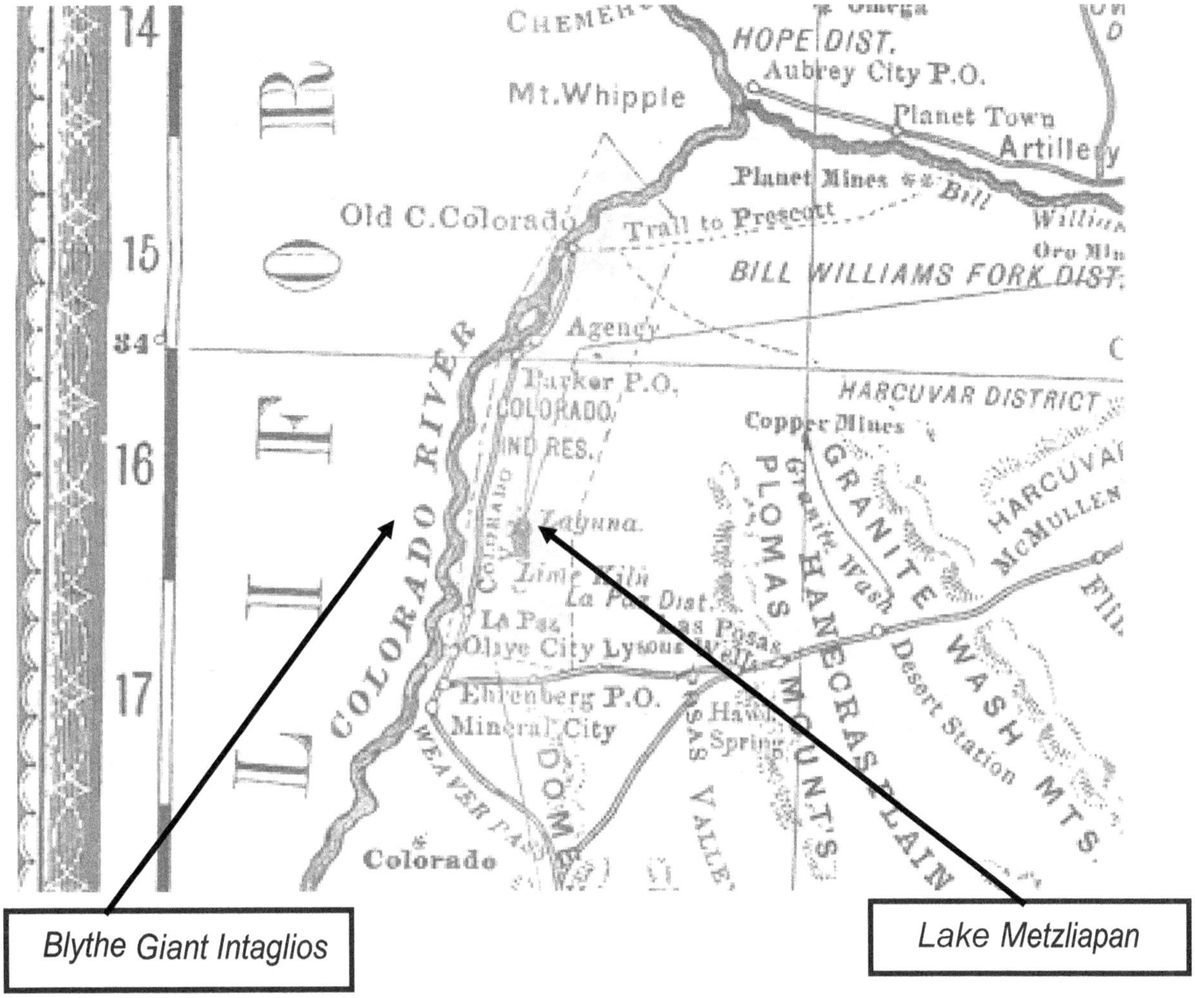

Blythe Giant Intaglios

Lake Metzliapan

1881 map shows the old lake which is called Whalia Hanyo by the Mojave which means Moon Lake in reference to the Moon Mountain adjacent to it and Lake Metzliapan by the Mexica. This is the same name of the lake that surrounded the Island of Tenochtitlan in Mexico City.

The Island of Aztlán was destroyed by the annual floods of the Colorado River leaving only the ruins of the vestige of some foundations that can be seen today.

The Blythe Giant Intaglios

Thousands of years ago, Indigenous people living in the Lower Colorado River Valleys created gigantic figures on the mesas throughout the desert and along the river. Archaeologists called them intaglios, an Italian term referring to an engraving process, while others called them geoglyphs, designs on the surface of the desert. The Blythe and Bouse figures, while technically geoglyphs are commonly referred to as intaglios, for our purposes are interchangeable.

Most geoglyphs were constructed on the dark gravel "desert pavement". The small stones of the desert pavement are dark because of their manganese stain. When the desert floor is not disturbed, you can picture it as a black board when seen from above. Those areas are so fragile and should be respected and not disturbed. To create an image on the desert mesas, the small cobblestones and gravel are scraped back to expose the light-colored caliche. The black cobblestones are placed outlining the image, exposing the caliche at the bottom layer, thus creating a lighter colored image. Most of the geoglyphs along the Lower Colorado River can be found within the 200 miles between Needles, Ca and Yuma, Az.

According to Boma Johnson, retired senior archaeologist of the Bureau of Land Management (BLM) in Yuma, "There are over 275 intaglios that have been identified up and down both sides of the Lower Colorado River. These include humans, animals, serpents, eagles and abstract geometric designs. BLM believes that they are 10,000 years old and have been found mostly on the Lower Colorado and Gila River Valley mesas, extending down to El Cerro del Pinacate, in Northwest Sonora, Mexico. They can also be found in the southern hemisphere near Cuzco, Peru in the Nazca plains where a similar method was utilized by the ancient nations." The most famous and most impressive of these unique geoglyph formations are the Blythe Giant Intaglios located 15 miles north of Blythe off U.S. Hwy 95. They are visited annually by tourists and curiosity seekers that come to marvel and study the enormous figures. The intaglios are numbered among the world's ancient mysteries and have been featured worldwide. They were also included in the National Register of Historic Places in Washington D.C. after a lengthy qualification process which first began in 1978. (Johnson, 1985).

The Blythe Giant Intaglios first appeared in the London News in 1932, (Palmer, 1932) and in September's 1952 issue of National Geographic Magazine which featured two articles titled, "Giant Effigies of the Southwest," by Army General George C. Marshal and "Seeking the Secrets of the Giants," by Frank M. Setzler. We were very fortunate to have communicated with Ellis N. Palmer, George Palmer's son and he provided us with copies of the original London Newspaper articles and other material. Since then, these famous intaglios have been featured in various journals, magazines, books, newspaper articles and documentaries.

One of the most well-known documentaries is "Chariots of the Gods," by Erich Von Daniken. In this documentary, he states, "that because the figures are best viewed from the sky, the natives perhaps were trying to communicate with people from outer space." Von Daniken's theory was not too erroneous in suggesting that the Blythe Giant Intaglios were trying to communicate with outer space. Our research reveals that the precise placement of the human figures illustrates the duality representing humans here on earth with their cosmic counterparts. There is a giant human image in the Vaticanus

A Codex that represents the giants that roamed the earth during the First Sun as shown in the Aztec Sun Stone calendar. The Sun is Called Ocelotonatiuh and its nahualli (animist) is the jaguar. These were the giants that were alive during that time and the old peoples' greeting was, "Don't fall because whoever fell would fall for good."

The Blythe Giant Intaglio of Ometeotl represents the giant human image in the Vaticanus A codex. The Blythe Giant Intaglio site is strategically located within the confines of the Omeyocan Diamond of Infinity which in the Nahuatl language means "Ome"(two), -"yo" (yollotl-heart) and "can"(place), place of the two hearts.

Omeyocan represents the place where the Nahua Creation Story originated and where Ometeotl, the Creator dwells. The Intaglios are located off U.S. Hwy 95 on a dirt road which goes up a small grade to a small knoll and in less than 250 yards the first of the giant figures is located. It represents the male of the three large human figures.

Ill 10

Ometeotl, Blythe Giant Intaglio

Ill 11
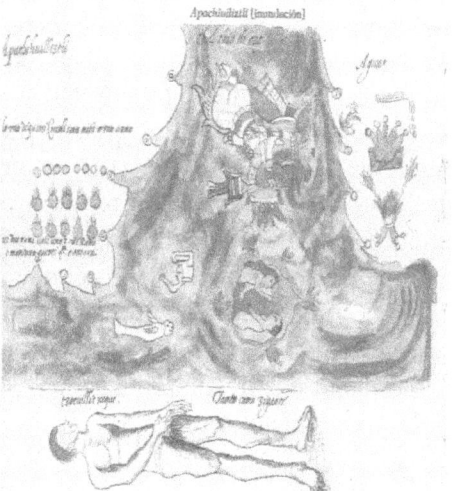
Vaticanus A Codex, Giant in the First Sun

The male figure in Nahuatl is called Ometecuhtli; "Ome" (two) and "tecuhtli" (male). Ometecuhtli is identified by the male organ and by the geometric position of his head towards the north and his arms extended in a form of a bow. His body therefore serves as the arrow, thus creating the bow and arrow image. Very faintly is a large circle that crosses his thighs which represents the universe. Ometecuhtli's image on earth represents the male and his counterpart duality is Orion in the cosmos. The line that passes through his thighs represents Orion's belt. Southeast of the male figure is a geoglyph image of the dog which has a long snout, pointed ears and a long neck. The dog is the nahualli of the male. It represents Xolotl, the twin of Ehecatl (wind) and together they are the Evening and Morning star which is Venus (Quetzalcoatl). The dog's counterpart in the cosmos is "Canis Major" that is Orion's (the hunter) companion.

In the Mexica Creation Story, Xolotl accompanies the Sun after the sunset. The image of the dog lead human spirits through the underworld where their rest in Mictlan as referred to in the codex. Below the dog image is a double-linked spiral image. The combination of the spirals symbolizes water, earth and fire, "A-Tla-Chinolli", "A"-water, Tla-talli/earth, Chinolli-fire/cosmos. All three represent the communicator, "Yeitiliztli" (the trinity). A-Tla-Chinolli's image is beside the eagle's beak as shown in the original Mexica flag before the Spanish Invasion and not as it is currently shown in the Mexican flag with a snake in the eagle's beak. The small spiral of the A-Tla-Chinolli image is pointed toward the river and aligns straight east to the Bouse Fisherman Intaglio. The larger spiral represents fire which is aligned with the west toward the pyramid shape of Marie Peak (in the Big Maria Mountains). Together the two spirals connected in an upright vertical position create an image of an hourglass. The small bottom spiral is represented by a seashell which represents the ocean/earth while the larger spiral represents the Milky Way in the cosmos. Thus, the male human figure intaglio, the dog and the double-linked spiral lie in a cluster on the first small knoll.

South, across an arroyo there is a second larger human figure that lies with another quadruped image that is on a small knoll. This is the largest of the three, measuring 171 feet from head to toe. It is the female, Omecihuatl, "Ome" (two) and "Cihuatl" (female). This intaglio has the similar position with the head and the arms resembling a bow and arrow as the other intaglio. Omecihuatl is identified by her bulging stomach like that of a woman that has just given birth with the placenta coming down her crotch. She is appropriately positioned with her head pointing south and with her stomach facing east toward the Moon Mountains across the Colorado River on the CRIT Reservation. Omecihautl represents the female on earth with its counterpart Cassiopeia in the cosmos. Cassiopeia's image is seen in the cosmos as a woman reclining in a chair and looking into a mirror that is in her hand. The constellation's main bright stars form a big "W" that is spread out and symbolizes the female's breasts. On earth the upside-down "W" is seen as an "M". The same image of the female breasts in the Milky Way is seen among several geoglyphs in the area that represents the woman, Mother Earth. To the south of the female figure on the same knoll is another animal image that is "Ocelotl" which is from the cat family. It has a square head, wide-open jaw and a short neck. Its counterpart in the cosmos is the Big Dipper constellation.

The European interpretation of the Big Dipper is a bear called "Ursa Major." However, among the Indigenous, it represents Ocelotl because of the black spots that it has on its body representing the stars. The cat family is associated with the female while the dog is associated with the male.

Continuing west on the dirt road passing the male human figure about 200 yards on another small knoll on a higher elevation is the third human figure which lies by itself. His head is pointing southwest and his arms extend similar to the other human images which represent a bow and arrow.

This image represents Ometeotl, "the Creator," "Ome" (two) and "Teotl" (energy) or "Two Energies." Ometeotl represents the male and female energies combined. This figure does not have the female or male organ but is the conception of both spirits. The female image that is southwest of the male figure is located southeast of the Ometeotl human figure. This positioning of the figures forms a triangle, an arrowhead that is pointing toward Marie Peak in the Big Maria Mountains. The three human figure intaglios are the principle factors in the Nahua Creation Story. They are another illustration of the Indigenous beliefs in the importance of the three energies: Ometecuhtli, Omecihuatl and Ometeotl, the Creator. All together, they form "Yeitiliztli," the sacred three.

The belief is similar to the Christian theology's Holy Trinity, the Father, Son and Holy Spirit. However, in the Mexica cosmic tradition, the woman is identified as one of the three main energies. On the walls surrounding the ancient Teocalli (temple) of Tula, Hidalgo, there are engraved images of the jaguar and dog glyphs which wrap around the temple wall. They are shown following each other all around the temple wall and are found among many ancient ruins throughout Mexico. The dog always has its tail down representing the male organ and its image is formed with the tail parallel to his rear legs. The jaguar, on the other hand, has an extremely long tail that loops down, then up creating a "U" shape. The "U" shape symbolizes the woman's womb and is also a glyph that represents Tezcatlipoca. (Waters, 1984)

The Blythe Giant Intaglios dog and jaguar figures originally had their tails in the same manner. However, the jaguar's tail was redesigned with good intentions in 1957, but unfortunately distorting its original formation which should be a "U" shape. In 1957, Mr. Collis Mayflower, chairman of the Blythe Chamber of Commerce Committee, provided most of the funding for fencing and restoration of the Blythe Giant Intaglios. Mrs. Kirk Brimhall and Mrs. Wayne Dill of the Parent Teacher Association and over 15 students of Palo Verde High School participated in this historical restoration event. Unfortunately, neither the Bureau of Land Management (BLM) nor the local tribes were involved in the restoration (Desert Magazine, 1957)

A Blythe teacher by the name of DeWeese W. Stevens volunteered to supervise the restoration and the students. They however, did not know that the Jaguar had a "looping tail." He and the students therefore arranged the images according to their own assumptions, and rearranged some of the human figures feet, and destroyed part of their heads and headdresses. According to Ron Van Fleet in the Mojave's interpretation, the Jaguar's tail was supposed to be arranged in the form of a "U." Van Fleet also stated that there were other programs at Palo Verde College in the early 1970s such as the Colorado River Guides, whose main purpose was to restore some of the geoglyphs west of Blythe, including the giant Kokopilli geoglyph, and numerous other sacred sites currently being threatened by solar power plants. It was hoped that tourist sites throughout the valleys would eventually be established and tour guides would come from the reservations. Throughout the years many other images have been destroyed forever by careless off-road vehicles and people trampling over them because of their lack of understanding and lack of respect for these indigenous symbols that represent the Creation story. It is very important for us to recognize the efforts of the people that participated in the first restoration event and the fencing of the Blythe Giant Intaglios. Without a doubt, they would have been destroyed long ago. Regardless of the distortion that took place during the fencing we will forever be grateful for their dedication and involvement.

Moon Mountain Twin Peaks

Ill 12

The twin peaks of the Moon Mountains that are facing west above the Parker Valley represent the vulva of Mother Earth. The Moon Mountains are just above the Island of Aztlán. South of the twin peaks, you see the "U" of the Plomosa Mountains where the moon rises during the equinoxes.

Ill 13

During the sunrise of the Spring Equinox, the sun rays shine between the twin peaks

During the spring equinox, the first sun rays of the rising sun shine between the twin peaks of the Moon Mountains, impregnating Mother Earth. Then the sun rays shine directly on Marie Peak on the ridge of the Big Maria Mountains. Marie Peak has the image of the pyramid called Tonatiuhichan and south of it is the profile image of the head of Huitzilopochtli looking south. Huitzilopochtli represents the sun. The Vindobonensis Codex, Fold 23 has his image with the sun in the background. North of Tonatiuhichan is the profile image of Cihuatcoatl facing north toward Topock Maze (Mictlan).

Vindobonensis Codex, Fold 23 Glyph Related to the Moon Mountain Twin Peaks

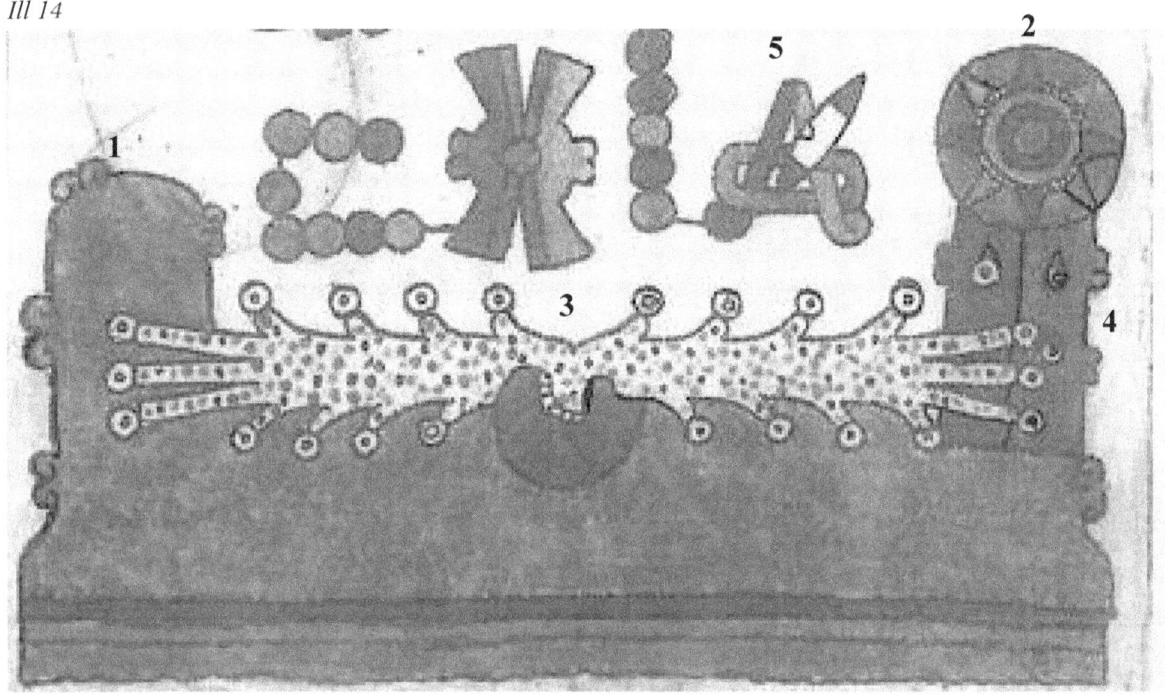

Ill 14

The twin peaks in the Moon Mountains (1) with the sun rising, (2) during the spring equinox. Also shown is the Alkali Lake (3) representing Lake Mexico that surrounded the Island of Aztlán. (4)The dark represents dawn before sunrise and the red represents the sunrise. (5) Year 5 Flint, 8 Day (beads), 4-Movement (Nahui-Ollin), the beginning of the First Sun of the Aztec Sunstone calendar. The eight movements represent the four directions on the northern hemisphere and the four directions in the southern hemisphere during the equinox.

Sun Impregnating Mother Earth Petroglyph

Ill 15

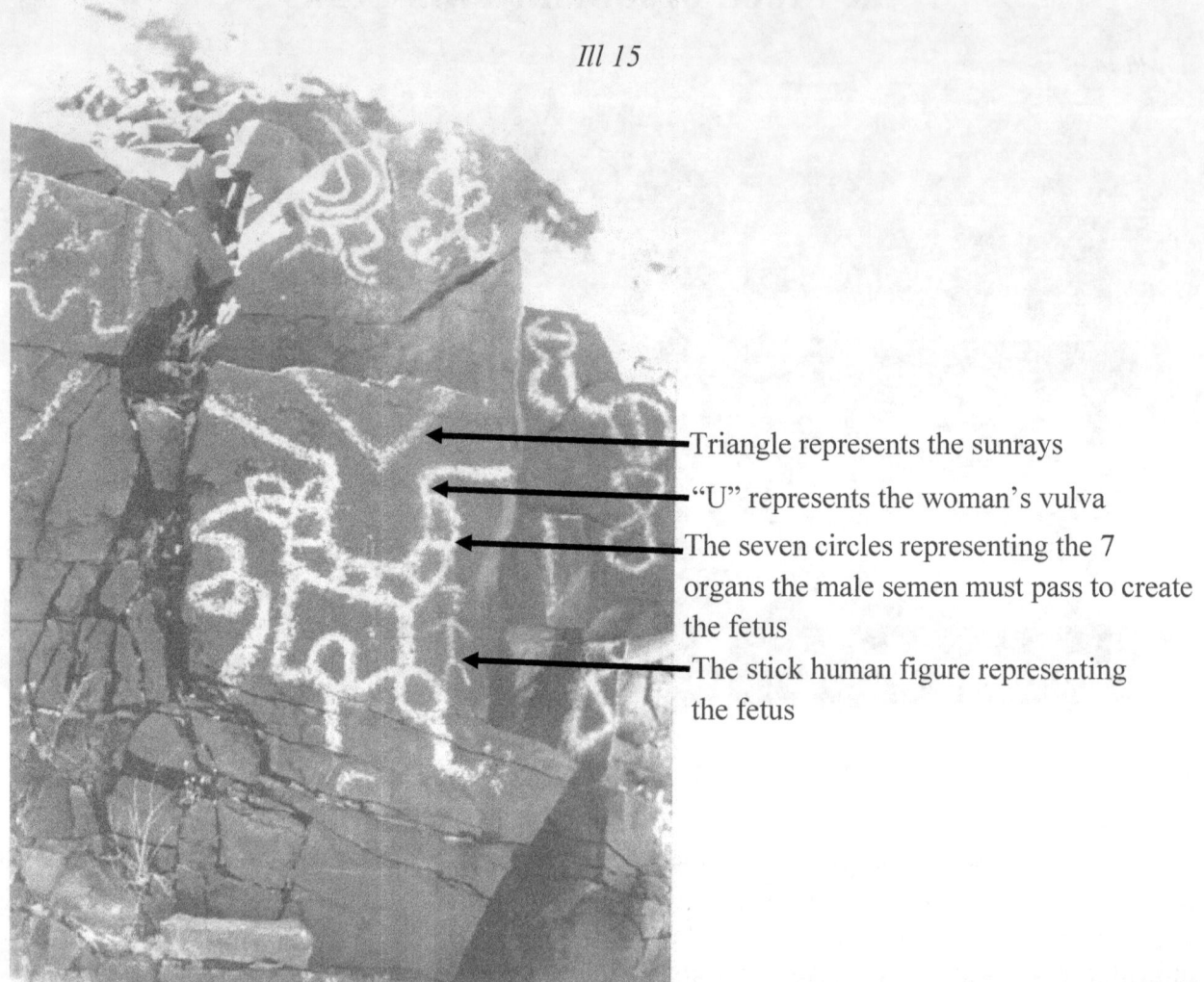

- Triangle represents the sunrays
- "U" represents the woman's vulva
- The seven circles representing the 7 organs the male semen must pass to create the fetus
- The stick human figure representing the fetus

These petroglyphs represent Xicomoztoc, place of origin of the Azteca/Mexica as described in the Historia Tolteca-Chichimeca codex. This is the metamorphosis of the impregnation of the woman during the spring equinox. The Father (Sun) is impregnating Mother Earth. The triangle represents the sun rays rising during the equinoxes and the "U" represents the woman's womb. The seven circles represent the seven organs the semen must pass to fertilize the woman to form the fetus. The stick human figure represents the fetus, humans born on earth.

Xicomoztoc-Place of Birthing of Humans
Historia Tolteca-Chichimeca Codex, Fold 16

Ill16

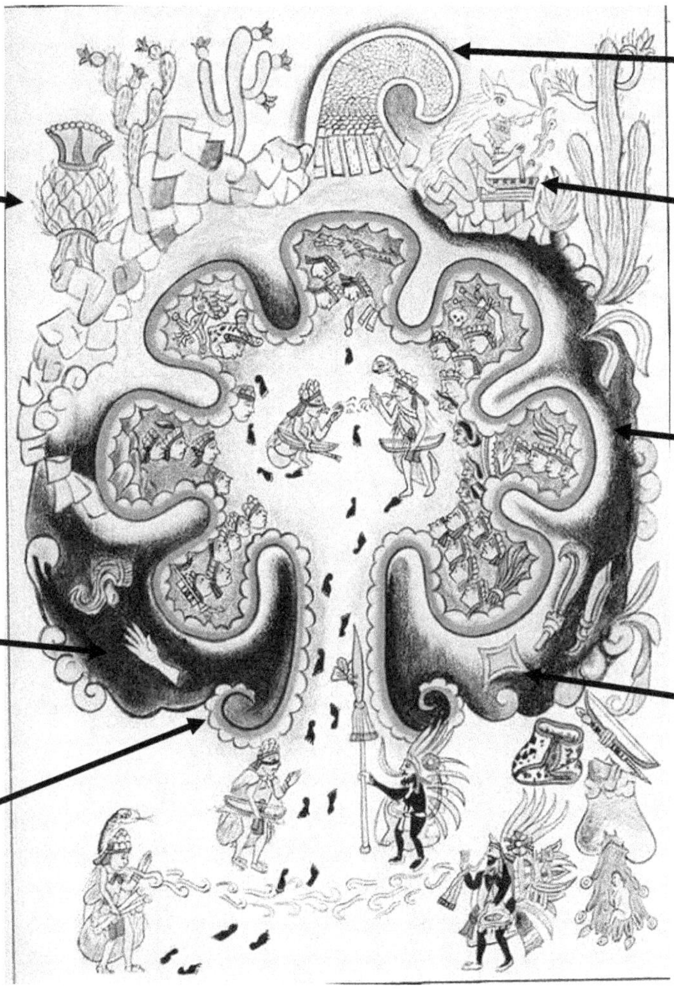

- Curved Mountain Peak refers to Teoculhuacan and the turtle's tail
- Bisnaga Cactus represents the cosmos and the thorns represent the stars
- Beginning of the New Fire Ceremony
- The 7 semi-circles representing the organs the male semen must pass before fertilization takes place
- The right hand of the Creator Tloque-Nahuaque
- Omeyocan Diamond-The Place of Two Hearts that overlays all the Parker Valley and the northeast Palo Verde Valley
- Woman's Vulva

The footprints in the codex image relate to the male semen. The man with spear represents the Sun (Tonatiuh) impregnating Mother Earth at Xicomoztoc on the Colorado River during the summer solstice. The Nahualli of Xicomoztoc is the beehive of human creation. The bee on the spear is going to the beehive to take pollen to the queen bee. The Mojave called it Thaampo Nyava (beehive). The footprints go to the seven organs (semi-circles) before becoming the embryo. That is why the footprints on the right are going in. The footprints on the left are coming out when you are born.

Historically speaking, the Xicomoztoc glyph has erroneously been referred to as the seven caves when in fact, they represent the seven organs of the woman's womb.

Comparison of Petroglyph and Codex

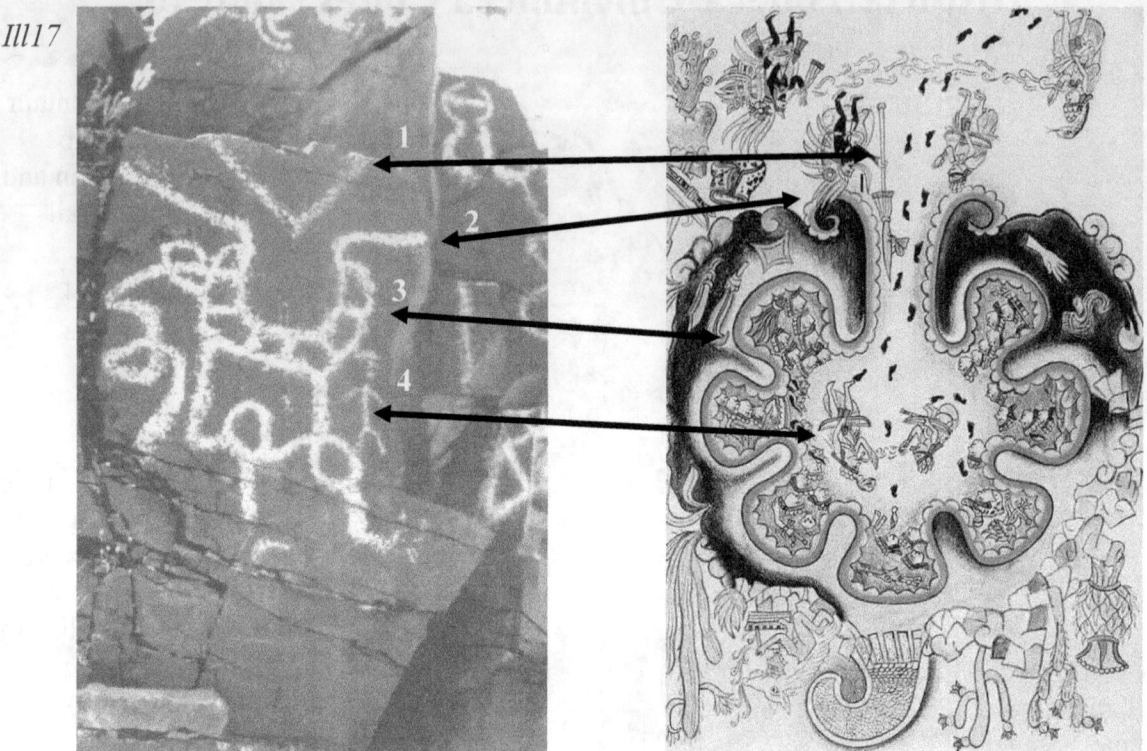

Comparison of the petroglyph with the Historia Tolteca-Chichimeca Codex

1. The sun rays (represented by the arrow n the petroglyph and by the spear in the codex) during the spring equinox that represents the impregnation of Mother Earth by Father Sun.
2. The "U" represents the woman's womb.
3. The seven circles represent the seven organs the male semen passes through to create the fetus.
4. The fetus.

Azcatitlan Codex Glyph of Xicomoztoc

Ill 18

Azcatitlan Codex, Fold 5- Xicomoztoc, the birthing of humans

1. Feline (Ocelotl) represents Mother Earth. 2. Bisnaga cactus (the nahual) represents the cosmos. 3. Huitzilopochtli in the form of Huitzilin, the hummingbird, represents the Sun and he has the spear that represents the sun ray that impregnates Mother Earth. 4. Woman representing Mother Earth. 5. Humans being born in Xicomoztoc 6. Calli (house)

Ill 19

1. The shadowed feline (Ocelotl) represents Mother Earth. 2. Tezcatlipoca's human face is looking up and west. 3. Xochitlpilli, the navel of earth connection with the cosmos.
These shadow mountain images are seen during the afternoon on the southeast side of the Big Maria Mountain Range during the winter solstice.

Images of the Meaning of Mexico

Xochitlpilli, the Navel of the Earth

Ill 20

The south end of the Big Maria Mountains shows the navel of Earth from where the name of Mexico comes. The photo was taken from the Arizona side of the Colorado River during the spring equinox. Mexico is translated: Me-Meztli (Moon), Xi-Xictl (Umbilical, Center) and Co (Place); the center of the moon. (Photo taken by Alfredo A. Figueroa)

Ill 21

The Tlaltecuhtli Idol represents the birth of Tezcatlipoca from the navel of the earth. 1. The navel of the earth, 2. Tezcatlipoca, 3. The spirit world

Ill 22

The rabbit is on the moon (shaped like an "olla.") The opening represents the vulva. The navel is shown with umbilical cord hanging (from the Mexica Codex).

White Limestone Eagle Image-Mixcoatcuauhtli

Ill 23

White limestone eagle in the Big Maria Mountain Range overlooking the Palo Verde Valley. 1. Head of the Eagle looking east to the sunrise with his wings spread out and his legs landing on top of Tepetl. 2. Black schist represents Tepetl (Rock) where the eagle lands as shown on the Mexican flag. 3. Shadow image of Huehueteotl, the old image of the Creator. (Photo by Alfredo A. Figueroa)

Ill 24

When the Mexica founded Mexico/Tenochtitlan, the site was built to emulate the eagle image in the Big Maria Mountains Range. El Templo Mayor in Tenochtitlan is called El Zocalo (place of the mud). El Templo Mayor was built on a man-made island in the middle of Lake Mexico. On the contrary, the eagle in the Big Maria Mountain Range is solid rock but the emulation in Mexico (El Templo Mayor) was constructed on a man-made island.

Aztlan, Land of the Whiteness

Ill 25

The whiteness of the Big Maria Mountain Range as seen from West Blythe, Acacitli. (Photo by Alfredo A. Figueroa)

Ill 26

Panoramic view of the whiteness of the Big Maria Mountain Range (Coatepetl) as seen from West Blythe, Acacitli. (Photo taken by Alfredo A. Figueroa)

One of the main references to what Aztlán is "Land of the Whiteness" because of the large white limestone images seen on the side of the mountains. The white limestone is an important part of the Creation Story as it represents the cosmos and the dark rocks represent Mother Earth. The image pf the snakes can be seen coming together. The image of the shield of Chimalma can also be seen. The black eagle is below the white limestone eagle.

In Search of Aztlán

The first documented search for Aztlán was recorded by Fray Diego Duran, in his book, *Historia Antigua de la Nueva España (Ancient History of New Spain)*. Duran wrote that Moctezuma Ilhuicamina, the fifth tlatoani (spokesperson of the Mexica from 1440 to 1469) wanted to know the location of Xicomoztoc/Aztlán, "the Place of the Seven Caves," which was the place where his ancestors originated. Moctezuma called the royal historian, the leader Cuauhcoatl (Eagle Serpent) and addressed him, "Oh Ancient Father, I desire to know the true story, the knowledge that is hidden in your books about the Seven Caves where our ancestors, our father and our grandfathers lived and whence they came forth. I wish to know about the place wherein our God, Huitzilopochtli dwelt and out of which he led our forefathers."

Moctezuma was so determined to seek the land that had given birth to the Azteca people that he sent his envoys north from the capital. Tenochtitlan (present-day Mexico City). When they returned, the envoys reported that they had fulfilled his orders and had seen the land called Aztlán/Xicomoztoc. (Chavero, 1976)

The Mexica Codex states that Huitzilopochtli was ordered by the Creator, Mecitli to leave Aztlán and guide the Azteca south. They were to change their name to Mexica in honor of the Creator Mecitli. Finally, after a journey that took approximately 200 years, in 1325, they settled in the region of the Valley of Anahuac.

After the Spanish conquest and the overthrow of the Mexica from Tenochtitlan in 1521, the Spaniards were intrigued with the rumors that they heard regarding a place called Aztlán, "A land of many riches." According to the legend, it was believed that there was a place known as the "Seven Cities of Gold of Cibola and Quivira" similar to the Mexica mystical place of Aztlán/Xicomoztoc, located northwest of Mexico/Tenochtitlan.

Hernan Cortes was the first Spaniard who was driven by greed in search of Aztlán and its riches. He left Acapulco and traveled toward Baja California Sur in search of his new venture. Unfortunately, Cortes only found a few pearls that he took from the natives. After Cortes' ill-fated venture to Baja California, the Spaniards were still excited by the many stories told of the riches that existed somewhere in the north.

In 1540, Francisco Vasquez de Coronado set out in his expedition in search of the fabled "Seven Cities of Gold" and "El Dorado" of Cibola and Quivira. He came up from Sinaloa through Sonora then followed the San Pedro River in Southern Arizona. There at the junction with the Gila River, Coronado sent his envoy, Melchor Diaz to search for Hernando de Alarcon. Alarcon was supposed to have traveled through the Gulf of California, up the Colorado River in order to bring Coronado supplies to continue his expedition.

Diaz traveled west along the Gila River to a point where the Halchidomas Trail intersected. He followed the trail all the way to the Colorado River to a point called Weaver's Pass on the Dome Rock Mountains (overlooking the Palo Verde/Parker/Cibola Valleys). Diaz came to the appropriately named Cibola Valley in search of Alarcon. He then continued down the river to Quechan territory near Yuma, Arizona. There he found a letter that had been left by Alarcon which explained that after waiting for him for a long time he decided to go back to Acapulco. Shortly after that, Melchor Diaz died in a freak accident across the Colorado River. Alarcon had traveled approximately 85 leagues up the Colorado River on his boat from the Gulf of California up to the area of present day Palo Verde/Parker Valleys.

In summary, Diaz and Alarcon were the first Spaniards to set foot in Aztlán approximately one hundred years after the people that were sent by Moctezuma Illuicaimina.

Following the European invasion, all historical writings in Mexico required a stamp of approval from the "Consejo Real de la Indias," the Spanish administrative office for New Spain.

For three hundred years, the history of Mexico was written and rewritten under the censorship and critical scrutiny imposed by the Spanish administrative office which was similar to the notorious Spanish Inquisition religious reactionary guidelines. Thus, very few truthful historical codices survived, including Vindobonensis, Borgia and Nuttall. This censorship has also made it difficult for many historians to accurately document Mexica cosmic and traditional history.

Despite the strict Spanish reviews, there are two documented writings of native life in Mexico during the 16th century. Both writings contain prudent pre-Cuauhtémoc historical Mexica history. The post-Cuauhtémoc codices have the most insidious denigrating version of the Mexica cosmic cultural traditions.

One of these writings was by Fray Diego Duran which was entitled *History of the Indias*. The other writing was by Fray Bernardino de Sahagun entitled *The Florentine Codex: General History of the things of New Spain*. During the Spanish Inquisition trials, Duran was a translator of Nahuatl to Spanish. Sahagun, on the other hand was determined at all cost to convert the natives from their cosmic cultural tradition to the European religion.

Fray Juan Zumarraga, the first bishop of Mexico, in his writings, boldly states with pride that he was personally involved in the burning of over 15,000 codices from the library of Texcoco, the main learning center of the Mexica.

Historians continue to insist on promulgating the centuries-old lies that portrayed the natives as savages, convincing the world that the Mexica practiced human sacrifices and that their cosmic cultural traditions were evil and their images of the Creator represented the devil. Today as researchers begin to analyze the writings related to the history of Indigenous people, they are uncovering many serious misrepresentations attributable to the Hispanicized Indigenous writers of the Era of New Spain (1521-

1821). In relation to the floods, Fray Duran mentions in his writings that Aztlán was destroyed after the Mexica left. Today all that is left are some foundations that were located on higher elevations that the old dried up lake that surrounded it.

According to the "Handbook of Arizona," published in 1877, a pyramid was located 50 miles north of Ehrenberg, Az. It was built of hewn stones and each stone was about 20-36 inches squared and was 104 feet square at the base and 20 feet high. Old-timers of the area have no recollection of seeing the pyramid but had heard of its whereabouts in the valley. (Cook, 1985)

The pyramid was without a doubt the one shown in the first fold of the Boturini Codex called "Tira de la Peregrinacion" and in the Aubin Codex. Bothe codices show a pyramid on the Island of Aztlán in the middle of a lake.

Before the construction of the dams, every summer the Colorado River would flood. The river would change its course and wipe out everything in its path. Therefore, it is logical to conclude that the pyramid was destroyed by the floods.

In recent years, we have seen a renewed interest in the whereabouts of Aztlán. The Los Angeles County Museum of Art presented a magnificent exhibition entitled, "The Road to Aztlán." The exhibit ran from May 13 to August 26, 2001.

Virginia M. Fields writes in the text that accompanied the exhibit, "The Road to Aztlán, Art from a Mythic Homeland," "… In the 1960s, the concept of Aztlán became associated with the Chicano movement for cultural affirmation and civil rights. As a Chicano symbol and allegory, Aztlán represents an ancestral homeland patterned after the mystical site of origin of the Aztecs, thought to be located in the region now known as the American Southwest. As this volume documents, the concept of Aztlán continues to have resonance for succeeding generations of Chicano and Mexican artists."

This exhibition coincided with the Xicano Movement's quest for Aztlán. It focused on archaeological evidence depicting the interaction between southwest United States and Mexico. It also featured many genuine artifacts including sacred stone images that were brought from Mexico's Museo del Instituto Nacional de Anthropoligia e Historia. The most recent research on the subject of Aztlan was also present.

The Getty Museum in 2010 had an excellent exhibition of the Azteca. The Aztec Pantheon the Art of Empire, rediscovering the Ancient Mexico has resurrected the magnificent history of the Aztec/Mexica.

The Mexica Creation Story gains momentum as the world seeks the truth about our human existence on earth.

The Destruction of the Island of Aztlan

Throughout the years, the annual floods of the might Colorado River eventually destroyed all the ancient Azteca structures of the Island of Aztlán in the Parker Valley, 25 miles northeast of Blythe, leaving only the vestige of the foundations that are found there today.

After Mexico lost the war with the United States in 1848, the Sonoran miners were ousted from the surrounding area of Sonora, California, during the Gold Rush of 1849. Most miners were force to leave their placer mines and most of them did not have any choice but to return to Sonora, Mexico. Most of the Sonora miners that remained behind were killed by Anglo miners who quickly took ownership of the gold mines. These types of barbaric events brought about the rising of Joaquin Murrieta and his guerilla fighters who rose in defense of the miners and against the United States fighting to regain California back to Mexico.

Later, in 1862, these ousted Sonoran miners from northern California were the same miners who first found the gold that led to the La Paz Gold Rush in the Colorado River. This quickly gave way to the new Gold Rush. The area of La Paz is located 10 mils northeast of Blythe, California, on the Colorado River Indian Tribes Reservation. Among the first to find gold in the area of La Paz, were the Contreras, Amavesca, Coz, Garcia, Farrar and other families including Teodosia Murrieta Martinez, the author's great-great grandmother.

The town of La Paz, Arizona, grew and the Mexican miners from Sonora, Mexico gathered up the stone foundations from the ruins of the Island of Aztlán to construct their homes and the town of La Paz. The ruins of the Island of Aztlán were approximately 10 miles north of La Paz. There, from the ruins of the Island of Aztlán, the miner brought the hewed stones that had been used for the teocallis in Aztlán and took them to La Paz to build the foundations of their adobe homes and building.

La Paz was a thriving river port town from 1862 to 1870. Steamboats from Santa Clara on the Gulf of California would go up through the delta of the river and stop in the Port of La Paz.

The Gold Rush of La Paz opened commerce to the area and was referred to as the "Gateway to the West." This brought about steamboats on the river bringing in businesses, transporting miners, mining equipment, soldiers and so on to Arizona, Nevada and southeast California. On the way back, the steamboats would take crude ore to Santa Clara on the Gulf and from there the ocean liners would take it to San Francisco, California.

In 1870, during the height of the flood, the river changed its course and completely destroyed the adobe houses and building structures of the town of La Paz. This destruction changed the geography of the river and forced the residents to relocate to higher ground, which today is the town of Ehrenberg, Arizona.

Today all that remains of La Paz are the small dirt mounds of adobe where the building once stood and the stone foundations that were brought from the Island of Aztlán.

Ill 27

A part of what remains of the Island of Aztlán, a native cottonwood tree with the egrets that do not want to leave. The tree is off Mojave Rd., north of the La Paz ruins. (Photo by Gilbert Leivas)

Aztlán: Consciousness in the Southwest

In reference to Moctezuma and Aztlán, there is an abundance of oral and physical evidence in the Lower Colorado River Valley. After the United States/Mexico War of 1846-48, Anglos who worked and lived in the area of the lower Colorado River Valleys became aware of Aztlán.

Oral traditionalists of the Opatas, Pimas, Papagos, and Yuman nations in Arizona and Sonora indicate that there is some traditional recollection of Moctezuma coming to their region/land and to the Lower Colorado River Valleys. This helps to confirm the lineage between most of the indigenous nations that made up the Confederation of Anahuac as described in the Mexica history.

After Mexico's War of Liberation from Spain in 1821, the new Mexican government began an extensive effort to reclaim its indigenous roots and the search for Aztlán continued. Moctezuma's memory remained strong in history and in 1827 there was a failed attempt to change the name of Alta California to Moctezuma which is today the state of California. (Gudde, 1959)

In the 1850s William H. Emory of the United States/Mexican Boundary Commission who traveled the area, wrote in his survey report that "The name Moctezuma was as familiar to every Pueblo, Apache and Navajo as the names of the Savor or George Washington was to the Anglo-Saxon."

When the first Arizona territory legislative assembly was held in Prescott in 1864, Governor John Goodwin's administration submitted a bill to call the new territory capital, "Aztlán." It was to be located in a town to be founded "at a point within 10 miles of the junction of the Verde River and Salt River."

The bill was not approved and the town of Phoenix was chosen instead to be the capital of the Arizona territory. "The site originally identified is within what is now Fort McDowell Reservation, northeast of Phoenix, 75 miles south of Arizona's geographical center, Clarkdale." (Wagner, 1980)

At one time Clarkdale was called Centerville for obvious reasons and was also named Romita by one of the Mexican resident families from Romita, Guanajuato, Mexico (Macias, 1954)

According to the University of Arizona Bulletin, "The Arizona Place", the state's first Masonic lodge in the City of Prescott, Arizona was named "The Aztlán Masonic Lodge". (1866) Continuing with the popular name of Aztlán, in 1877 there was the Aztlán Gold Mine and Aztlán Mill located in the surrounding mining area of Prescott. During that time, several novels were written about the "mystical" Aztlán.

Continuing with the name, Moctezuma, in 1902, it was proposed as the state name for the combined territories of Arizona and New Mexico. (Barnes, 1960)

Orgullo De Aztlán-Pride of Aztlán

During this present epoch, many books of the Xicano struggle have been written. One of the best books that briefly tells of the spiritual feeling and longing of knowing the truth of their ancestral Aztlán is *Orgullo de Aztlán (Pride of Aztlán)* by Esther Perez. In her book, she depicts the struggle beginning with Aztlán/Huehuetlapallan being above the confluence of the Gila and Colorado Rivers and the Mexica migration down to Mexico/Tenochtitlan. In the following text, we quote her dedication to future generations that expresses her thoughts.

"To the spirit of courage and nobility that has carried the greatness of our race forward from Aztlán and seen at last this proud return to ancestral soils.

To the long communion of perseverance that made up our people know patience. To the centuries of bondage which now forces us to grow more quickly, bursting with energies too long repressed and freedoms so long denied.

Finally, to each child of Aztlán, who looks into himself; and discovers an eagle's strength, and our Indian wisdom, and the knowledge to live proudly in the present."

Mexico/Aztlán on the Colorado River and Its Relationship to Mexico/Tenochtitlan

One must know how to interpret the Mexica codex and the origin of the name, Mexico to thoroughly understand the metaphoric symbolism of the Mexica Creation Story as it correlates to the images on the mountains, equinoxes, solstices, oral history, geoglyphs on the mesas and petroglyphs on the rocks in the surrounding Palo Verde/Parker Valleys.

During the migration from the Colorado River, it was common for the Nahua to look for similar locations, geographic conditions and images and name them in honor of their place of origin. This was done so they would remember and fulfill the Creator's principle to take this knowledge to all four directions. The names, Atotonilco, Aztlán, Culhuacan, Mexico and Tenochtitlan are good examples of the names which were duplicated during their migration to the four directions according to Dr. Alfonso Caso. An excellent analysis is given by Dr. Doris Heyden in her book, *Mexico Origin de un Simbolo*, as to why the name Mexico and Tenochtitlan. In her book, Heyden explains her verbal communications with Eduardo Mateos Moctezuma who state that "the land under the twin towers of La Plaza Mayor in Mexico City is all a swampland."

Heyden states that "this discards the possibility that there existed a rocky outcropping with a cave and a spring." The swampland at La Plaza Mayor was appropriately called "El Zocalo" meaning place of the mud. Zocalo deciphered is Zo-zoquete (mud), Cal-calli (house), O (place); house of mud (not of rock). This evidence totally disproves the government's position that Tenochtitlan was founded on a rocky outcropping on an island in Lake Mexico. It was supposed to have been where the eagle landed on top of a nopal (cactus) that grew from a rock outcropping.

As we analyze the evidence presented, the name Tenochtitlan was given to the island, not based on the finding of the swampland but based on the original Tenochtitlan. The name was brought with them when they came from the Colorado River.

The origin of the allegorical meaning of Tenochtitlan comes from the Big Maria Mountain Range on the Colorado River. Tenochtitlan deciphered is Te-tetl (rock), Noch-nopalli (cactus), Ti (binding), Tlan (place); "the place where the cactus grew on the rock."

In the Big Maria Mountain Range overlooking the Palo Verde Valley, is a large white limestone image of the thunderbird eagle. Its wings are spread out over a half mile aligned east and west. The head is turned facing east toward the Moon Mountains where the sun rises on the CRIT Reservation. This thunderbird eagle image is seen from West Blythe and the image of the thunderbird eagle appears to straddle a small dark peak. This is symbolic to the eagle that landed on the nopal (cactus) and refers to Tenochtitlan.

This image is seen today on the Mexica flag and has been on all their flags and banners for thousands of years to remind them of the Creation Story, their place of origin on the Colorado River. The only

time that this image was not used was during the 300-year occupation of the Spanish invaders that lasted from 1521-1821. This image is on the artifacts that have been found while digging in El Zocalo. The importance of the thunderbird eagle is well manifested among the Native art in the United States and Mexico. The thunderbird eagle's nahualli is Mixcoatcuauhtli (Cloud-Snake-Eagle, represents the Milky Way).

Alluding to the sacredness of the eagle image of the Big Maria Mountains is the location of the ancient destroyed Island of Acacitli. Acacitli means jackrabbit in the tulles and was called Barrio de La Liebre by the old Spanish-speaking Chemehuevi and other Indigenous people. Today, Acacitli is called Barrio Cuchillo in West Blythe.

The following is a translation from the book, *Tres Cientificos Mexicanos* by Ignacio Bernal, who states "I consider that the inscriptions on the rocks are the most genuine source of knowledge in the manner of thinking of the ancient Natives. Likewise, are paintings that in reality are very few that have been discovered on the monuments. In both cases, they are absolutely authentic data that shows the thinking of the Indigenous. You can incur an error by the wrong interpretation of the inscriptions or because the scribe was mistaken."

Ignacio Bernal and Alfonso Casa are two of the most renowned investigators of the Aztec culture.

Mexico is a nation deeply rooted in its cosmic traditional culture since time immemorial. The Confederation of Anahuac extended from the Rocky Mountains in the north to Nicaragua (meaning up to here came the Nahua). That is why we must know its history to understand its origin. As stated previously, the cosmic moral of the Mexica is the base of all societies.

The First Sunrise
The Beginning of the First Sun
of the Azteca/Mexica Creation Story

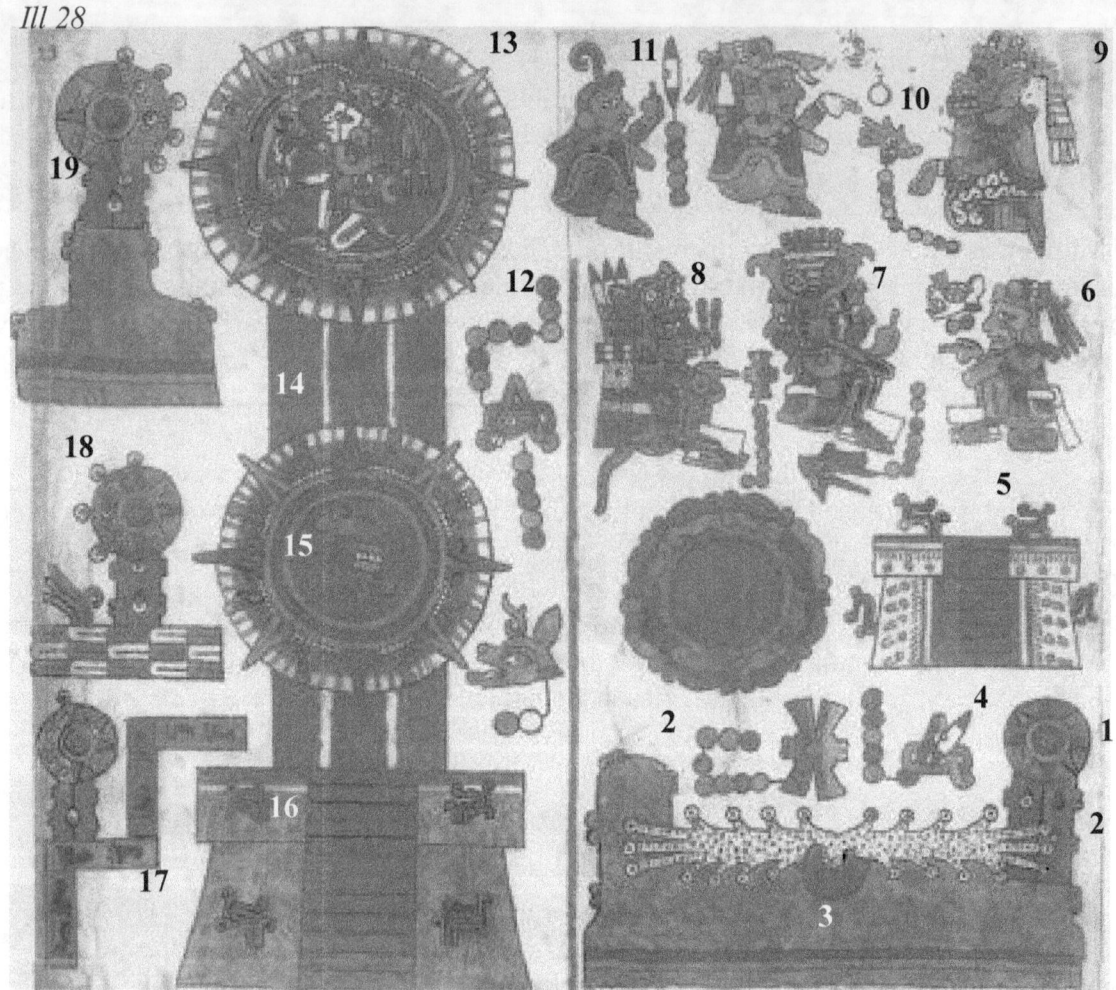

Ill 28

The Vindobonesis Codex depicts the area where the Blythe Giant Intaglios are located. Across the Colorado River are the twin peaks of the Moon Mountains on the Colorado River Indian Tribes Reservation (CRIT). This codex identifies the beginning of the spring equinox that in reference is the beginning of the First Sun on the Aztec Sunstone calendar (Tonalmachoitl). It shows the images of the heads of Huitzilopochtli and Cihuatcoatl on the Big Maria Mountain Range. The Vindobonensis Codex is pre-Hispanic and is, without a doubt, one of the few codices that relates the true Mexico Creation Story.

Deciphered Images of the First Sun in the Vindobonensis Codex, Fold 23 are as follows:

1. The sunrise during the spring equinox
2. The Moon Mountain Twin Peaks on the CRIT Reservation
3. Dried up alkalized Lake Metzliapan (Lake Mexico) where the Island of Aztlán was, at the base of the Twin Peaks.
4. Year 5 Flint, 8 Day-4 Movement, beginning of the First Sun on the Aztec Sun Stone calendar.
5. Meseta altar hill, east of dried lake at the base of the Moon Mts, has 9 steps referring to the transition of the 9 levels of the underworld that have risen during the sunrise.
6. 2 Dog, Xolotl (Evening Star) advising Quetzalcoatl
7. Lord 7, Wind (Ehecatl), Quetzalcoatl, Eagle with 3 faces
8. Señor 7 Movement Precious Jaguar (Mother Earth)
9. Cihuatcoatl 9 Weed Woman representing the duality of Huitzilopochtli
10. Converses with Nana, Lady, 1 Eagle
11. And with Lady, 5 Flint, Maiz/Corn, Flower
12. Year 13 Rabbit, Day 2 Deer was the sacred date
13. Tonatiuh, Huitzilopochtli's image looking south during the first sun ray that shines on his profile face on the Big Maria Mt ridge during the spring equinox.
14. The reddish color represents the rising sun & the morning shadow going down from the Big Maria Mt Ridge.
15. The sun continues to rise & the sunlight reaches the foothill of the Big Maria Mt, merging the unity of water, earth's surface and fire (cosmos). A-Tla-Chinolli
16. Finally, the morning sunlight reaches the Altar of the World facing east, the 13th level of knowledge. It is at the western end of where the last of the Blythe Giant Humanoid Intaglios are. Standing at the altar, looking southeast, you can see the winter solstice at Dome Rock Mt across the river. Looking east you can see the fall & spring equinoxes on the Moon and Plomosa Mts Twin Peaks & looking northeast you can see the summer solstice on Battleship Peak at Buckskin Mt.
17. The Sun has risen and Night is leaving and the migration leads to the 4 directions as shown by the footprints.
18. The Sun rises on the desert plains of the Chuckawalla Valley that reaches the Tulles of Corn Springs (Tula) in the Chuckawalla Mountains, east of the Intaglios.
19. Finally, the Sun begins to set and brings the night on the Eagle Mountain range.

1847 Map of Mexico, Used for Treaty of Guadalupe Hidalgo

Ill 29

In 1804, the eminent German cartographer and historian, Alexander Von Humboldt drew a map of what was at that time called New Spain which included present day Mexico and Southwest United States. Von Humboldt, however, never traveled to the Lower Colorado River Valleys so his informants must have given him the information and copied some earlier maps. The information of some sites mentioned is fairly close to the actual localities in the Lower Colorado River Valleys such as Concepcion, Antigua Residencia de los Azteca referring to Aztlán.

This was the official map of Mexico in 1847 that was used in the signing of the Treaty of Guadalupe Hidalgo by the United States and Mexico on February 2, 1848. Mexico lost more than half of their original territory which included Aztlán.

Zoomed Treaty of Guadalupe Map on the Colorado River

Ill 30

1. Concepcion (Conception Point) of the Creation Story, Antigua Residencia de los Aztecas
2. Chemeguaba Indian Tribe is now known as the Chemehuevi Tribe
3. The approximate true location of the Conception Point in the Parker Valley
4. Ruinas de las Casas Segundas de los Aztecas

The map clearly shows Antigua Residencia de los Azteca" (ancient residence of the Aztec) located at a junction on the Colorado River called "Concepcion" (Conception) meaning beginning. This is the first indication on a map alluding to the location of Aztlán. The map confirms that Aztlán was truly on the Colorado River. The true location of Concepcion is in the Parker Valley. Between Concepcion and Rio Santa Maria is Chemeguaba Indios (now Chemehuevi). Traveling southeast on the map, on the Gila River is "Ruinas de las Casas Segunda de los Azteca (Ruins of the second house of the Aztec), the first stop of the Aztec migration. The geographic location of the ruins is today, approximately the same location of the Casa Grande National Monument in Arizona. Continuing southeast to the State of Chihuahua, Mexico is "Casas Tercera de los Azteca" (third house of the Aztec) which today are the Ruins of Paquime in Casas Grandes, Chihuahua, Mexico.

Chimalma's Face Image on the Big Maria Mountains

Ill 31

The most outstanding image of Chimalma is located on the south side of the Big Maria Mountain. Next to the white eagle image on the right is an exceedingly large shield-like white limestone face image that begins at the base of the mountainside. It goes half way up the mountainside and it is embedded and surrounded by the dark wollastinite mineral that make the shield outstanding when seen from Acacitli (West Blythe). The shield in Nahuatl is called Chimali. The limestone shield image represents Chimalma (Mother Earth) and is the mother of Quetzalcoatl on Mother Earth. She is the image of the shield because it represents defender of Mother Earth.

In the first fold of the Boturini Codex, the migration from Aztlán shows the two persons at the bottom of the Island of Aztlán are Chimalma and Quetzalcoatl. Chimalma is identified by her shield and her hairdo.

In the third fold of the same codex, Chimalma is shown as one of the four sacred bundle carriers (Teomamas) leaving Aztlán

Chimalma as a Teomama Leaving Aztlán

Chimalma with her shield as one of the four Teomamas carrying the bag of knowledge to the four directions -Boturini Codex, Fold 3

Chimalma (left) with her shield and Quetzalcoatl, her son at the base of the Island of Aztlán-Boturini Codex, Fold 1

Chimalma's images can be seen in different forms, petroglyphs in Texas and idols down among the Maya in Yucatan to remind them of Chimalma's place of origin on the Big Maria Mountains.

Chimalma's Idol image in the Mayan culture is called Mah K'ina Yax K'uk'Mó, the Divine Lord of Copan.

Chimalma shield pictograph at Painted Rock, Texas. During the day of the winter solstice, a dagger of sunlight will slide across a steep bluff on the banks of the Concho River. It is when the sun stands highest in the sky. The sunlight will shine across the shield. (Star Date Online, 12/20/2004)

Big Maria Mountain Range

Ill 36

View of the Big Maria Mountains from Blythe, CA (Photo by Alfredo A. Figueroa)

The Big Maria Mountain Range before the 1900s was called the Chemehuevi Mountains on the Topo map in reference to Chimalma, place of Chimalhuacan, place of the shield.

Later in the beginning of the last century, the name was changed to their present Big Maria Mountains and Little Maria Mountains. They were changed to Big Maria because Maria is the mother of Jesus Christ and they changed the name from Chimalma, the creator Quetzalcoatl's mother and translated to the Catholic Religion Doctrine.

This has been the policy of the Europeans since the Spanish Invasion of 1492, to obliterate all remnants of the Indigenous cosmic culture tradition and force them to accept the European religion.

The old Chemehuevi Spanish-speaking would call the four peaks of the Big Maria Mountain that are seen from the Colorado River Indian Tribes Reservation, "Las Cuatro Marias." They are represented as the Nahui Teomamas, the four knowledge carriers.

In the original Uto-Aztecan linguistic families, the Chemehuevi were called Chimahuevus. The Chemehuevi, Hopi, Tohono-Oodham, Pima, Opota and Mexica are all members of the Uto-Aztecan family.

According to Professor Jose Acamapixtli Garcia, a Nahuatlaca, the word Chemehuevi is derived from the Nahuatl origin Chimahuevus meaning Chimali (shield). "Chima" comes from Chimalli (shield). "Hue" comes from huey (ancient/grand). "Vus" comes from Nuhu (the people/the first born). In other words, Chimahuevus means the ancient people, the protectors as demonstrated in Fold 52 of the Vindobonensis Codex.

Up until the 1950s, the Mexicanized Spanish speaking Chemehuevi still called themselves Chimahuevus.

Ill 37

Zoomed Big Maria Mountain (Coatepetl in Nahuatl)

Francisco Garces, the Spanish priest that came with Captain Juan Bautista de Anza to the Colorado River in 1776 called the Chemehuevi, Chemegue and Chimeguaba.

Alexander Von Humboldt, the eminent German cartographer, in his 1804 map identifies the Chemehuevi as Chimeguaba, a nation living on the Colorado River below the Antiguas Residencias de los Aztecas.

A.L. Krober, in his book, Hand book of the Indians of California, on page 710 writes that the Digueños and Manias called the Chemehuevi, Chinuwowo.

In the 1850s, a Chemehuevi clan was living in the area of West Blythe called "El Barrio de la Liebre: "Jackrabbit," or neighborhood. It was called "Acacitli" in Nahuatl during the times the Azteca/Mexica were here. They lived along the old destroyed Island of Acacitli in half submerged huts in the morro bluffs called Jukis.

The east/west trail that passed through the Barrio de la Liebre was called Vedera de La Liebre (Jackrabbit trail). It is currently called Riverside Drive and goes to the west mesa. Going west from the west mesa it was called Coco- Maricopa trail. This same trail continues to Point Dume, Malibu on the Pacific Ocean. Malibu represents the land navel to the ocean.

Four Peaks of the Big Maria Mountains

Ill 38

Four Teomamas from the Boturini Codex, Fold 3

The four Big Maria Mountain Peaks as seen from the Colorado River Indian Tribes Reservation called "Las Cuatro Marias" by the Chemehuevi Elders. The four Teomamas (Boturini Codex) represent the four Big Maria Mountain Peaks. The footprints indicate the path taken. The lead Teomama is Tezcacoatl and is carrying Huitzilopochtli in the form of Huitzilin, the hummingbird. The second is Cuauhcohuatl (eagle serpent). The third in line is Apanecatl (water and rain) and the last in line is Chimalma (the mother of Quetzalcoatl that took all the knowledge when they left Aztlán).

The four mountain peaks are aligned in a north/south direction because the southern hemisphere of the world is just as sacred as the northern hemisphere. Cusco, Peru in the southern hemisphere is the duality of Mexico, the umbilical of the earth in the northern hemisphere.

There are other aligned 4 mountain peaks all over the southwest such as the peaks west of Tempe, Arizona and in Northern California there are the Joaquin Mountain Ridge four peaks. All these four peak mountain ranges depict the migration of the four Teomamas to the four directions of the world from the Big Maria Mountain Range.

Vindobonensis Codex, Fold 52-Prelude in the Sky
Beginning and Ordinance of the Cosmos

Ill 39

The first humans, Vindobonensis Codex, Fold 52

In the beginning, (1) it was the cosmos. (2/3) There was a sacred discussion of the creation of nature, the rocks, animals, etc. They (2 black spirits) offered tobacco and beverage (to mix together for the creation of civilization). (4) Nights were given and set. (5) Days were ordered and set, first there was obscurity all around, then the days were in file and counted. (6) The birthing and setting of Nuhu was ordered and the ending of humans. (7) The primary couple, Señor One Deer and Señora One Deer with its descendents.(translated from Origen E Historia de Los Reyes Mixtecos, libro explicativo del llamado Codice Vindobonensis).

The Vindobonensis Codex is one of the few codices that was not influenced by the Spanish Invasion and is pre-Cuauhtemoc.

The Birthing and Ending of Nuhu (The People)

Ill 40

Ill 41

It was ordered the birthing and the ending of life. The image on the left shows Nuhu being born from the womb of Mother Earth, Xicomoztoc. The image on the right shows Nuhu going down to the afterlife. The Creator is admonishing Nuhu with his finger because of his conduct during his life on Mother Earth

Nuhu (the people) is the first human on earth and is the protector of all cultivation. The name Nuhu is derived from the Mixteco language similar to the Chemehuevi name of Nuwu or Nuwui

Ill 42

North end, east side of McCoy Mountains, seen from the McCoy Valley, shadow image of Nuhu as he is born when he descends from Tamoanchan when seen during the winter solstice (Photo taken by Alfredo Acosta Figueroa)

Ill 43

Nuhu on the north end, east side of McCoy Mountains (2) on the left of Tamoanchan (1) which is on the right. (Photo taken by Alfredo Acosta Figueroa

Nuhu's image in the codex is similar to the actual mountain image of Nuhu seen on the McCoy Mountains. The image of Nuhu is seen at 3:00 in the afternoon during the winter solstice when the old year ends and the new year begins.

McCoy Mountain in Nahuatl is called Nonoalcatepetl which relates to Quetzalpetlatl laying on the mountain range. Nonoalcatepetl is translated to say, "laying stretched out in her house in the mountain." Quetzalpetlatl is the female duality of Quetzalcoatl. Nuhu represents the human spirit descending from the cosmos to Tamoanchan (Granite Peak), from the McCoy Valley looks like a giant pyramid.

The images on the mountains represent the cosmic spirituality and the intaglios (geoglyphs) represent the spirituality on earth. The spirituality of Nuhu is the geoglyph image of what we call El Tosco (Hefty) in Spanish. El Tosco's image is approximately 10 miles southeast of Nuhu image in the McCoy Mountain directly in line with Granite Peak.

Siguenza Codex, Migration from Aztlán

Ill 44

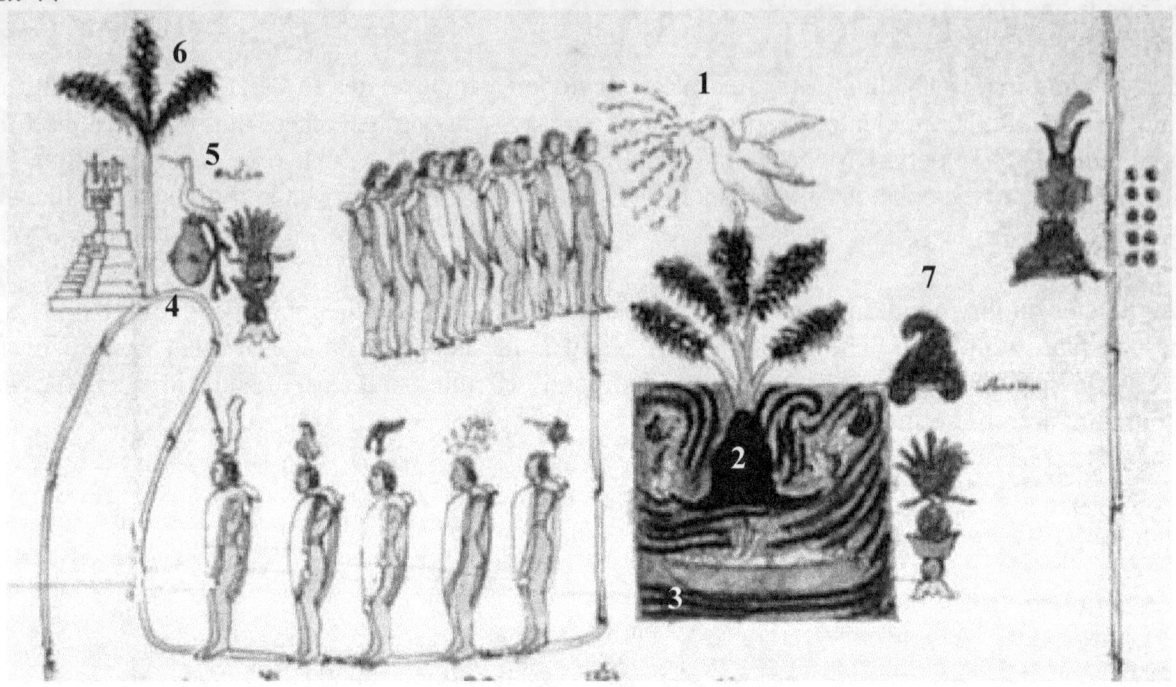

Siguenza Codex depicting the migration from Aztlán along the Colorado River to Mexico/Tenochtitlan

1. Mixcoatcuauhtli-The Eagle telling the Mexica to go take the knowledge from Tamoanchan. "Mexica Tihui, Tihui, Tihui, Tamoanchan." (Mexica, go find your home)
2. Aztlán Island, Parker Valley
3. Quetzalcoatl is leaving the Colorado River in a canoe
4. Olla represents Xicomoztoc
5. The Heron, a symbol of Aztlán
6. Yeitiliztli, the sacred three of the Creator, Omecihuatl, Ometeotl in the middle and Ometecuhtli, the tree of life, Tamoanchan.
7. Teoculhuacan, twisted peak on the Big Maria Mountains.

Codice Mexicanus

Ill 45

Códice Mexicanus, Lamina XVIII

The bird is on the tree that represents the Island of Aztlán on the Colorado river Indian Tribes Reservation. The bird is talking to the Mexica that are leaving Aztlán. It is saying Tihui, Tihui, Tamoanchan (Go find your house).

The Colorado River is flowing south. The other branch of water represents the old river channel that went west creating the Palo Verde Valley North Mesa.

There is a face to the left of the people inside Calli (house) that represents the Mule Mountain, 15 miles southwest of Blythe, as shown on the Aztec Sunstone Calendar.

The person in front of the trail with his hands up has a cactus staff telling the people to follow him. He represents Huitzilopochtli leading the Mexica from Aztlán during the migration. The other person that has a staff is the leader of the Teomamas, the bundle carriers of knowledge to the four directions (Nahui-Ollin).

The year 1168 is erroneous and does not correlate with the last 52-year cycle of November 15, 2003. 1067 is the date of the ending of the Third Sun of the Aztec Sunstone calendar, the year the Mexica left Aztlán.

The Bird Songs
Oral History of the Migrations from Aztlán

The Nahua Nations migrated to the four-directions (Nahui-Ollin) from the Lower Colorado River Valleys throughout thousands of years during the different eras. According to certain beliefs, the migrations began with the Azteca, continued with Olmeca, Zapoteca, Mixteca, Tolteca, Chichimeca, etc. The Mexica were last to migrate south to the Valley of Anahuac in the 12th Century.

During their journeys south, the Nations were assisted by the Creator. In his book, "Los Aztecas," Alfredo Clavero quotes Fray Torquemada saying that the Azteca/Mexica were led on their migrations by a bird that often appeared in a tree and repeatedly uttered a shrill cry (chillado) that sounded like Mexica Tihui-Tihui Tamoanchan meaning "Adelante Mexica, busca tu casa." (Mexica go forward, seek your house.)

Hearing the cry, the Mexica wise men, Hitziton and Tecptzan were compelled to follow the bird's command. Clavero adds that in Mexico, there is a bird known as Tihuitochan whose chillo (cry) translates clearly as "Vamos a nuestra casa (Lets go to our hose)." (Clavero, 1984)

Professor Carmen G. Basurto's book, *Mexico y Sus Simbolos* contains a play depicting the Mexica being led all the way from Aztlán to Tenochtitlan by a bird that shrilled "Tihui, Tihui" (forward, forward).

Mojave oral history includes songs about a bird leading the Hokan Nations thousands of years ago, coming from a place called Yucatan up to Spirit Mountain, Avi Kwame in Mojave (Ron Van Fleet) and Tlalocan in Nahuatl. (Alfredo A. Figueroa)

From a nearby tree, the bird would call out, "Thee-yem, Thee-yem Aha Makhav" (Mojave, go and find your destiny), shrilling the same song daily until they settled on the Colorado River at the base of Avi-Kwame (Spirit Mountain). (Steve Lopez, 1994)

The same bird that guided and led the Hokan families up to Spirit Mountain led the Uto-Azteca families down from the Colorado River to the Valley of Anahuac. This bird is depicted in the Siguenza and the Mexicanus codices and is calling the Mexica to follow him across the Colorado River. The bird is called Tildillo in Nahuatl and in English it is called the black-necked stilt. The scientific name is Himantopus Mexicanus. The bird is very common in the Lower Colorado River Valleys and breeds locally. Most of the time, it is seen out in the agricultural fields during irrigation. When they are in groups in a certain area, all you can hear is their loud shrilling that resembles "Tihui, Tihui" (Bert Anderson) It means go forward or follow me in Nahuatl. (Alfredo A. Figueroa)

According to former Bower Museum curator, Paul Apodaca, traditional bird songs are part of the Lower Colorado River Basin oral history. Recounting the migrations to the four directions, they are possible the oldest cultural songs in the hemisphere, hailing back thousands of years.

Other Native songs such as deer, fox, mountain sheep, the turtle and salt songs also have migration themes. These traditional songs are still sung in most of the traditional ceremonies throughout the Colorado River Basin and Mexico.

Petroglyph evidence indicates that many of the Lower Colorado River Nations that went south followed the Gila River from its junction with the Colorado River in Yuma, Arizona. Along the southward migration trail, the Heron petroglyph is first found near the town of Gila Bend, Arizona. The migrating nations reached this area either by following the Gila River from Yuma or by using the old Halchidoma trail that begins in the Palo Verde/Parker Valleys and ends in Gila Bend. The nations then continued to Casa Grande where according to Pima oral history, they constructed the large adobe structures, which today are known as Casa Grande National Monument. (Shaw, 1991)

Our records reveal that they left based on the computation of the traditional cultural cosmic 52-year New Fire Celebrations. The New Fire glyph is shown on top of the Teocalli of Aztlán in the Boturini Codex. The Seven Sisters geoglyph image is also among the Blythe Giant Intaglio geoglyph clusters.

Guided by Mecitli's prophecy attributed to Huitzilopochtli, the Nahua followed the same migration path used by the Herons and other migrating birds on their annual flight from the lakes of Central Canada and the Rocky Mountains down the Colorado River and south to Mexico. Most historians agree that all the Nahua families left from the same area at one time or another, each taking a different route. (Carpañia)

One of the first codices about the migration of the Tolteca was written by Hueman, a Tolteca traditional leader who reigned during the journey south from Aztlán. Hueman wrote the "Divine Book" in which he described the migration from the red region of Huehuetlapallan above the confluences of the Gila and Colorado Rivers. (Perez, 1972)

Most of the pre-Cuauhtémoc codices were destroyed by the European conquerors and over-zealous priests that viewed traditional indigenous images and beliefs as evil and viewed indigenous nations as worshipers of the devil. The European distortion and misinterpretation of the codices cast confusion upon the world and mystified the identification of the place from where the Nahua left on their journey south to Mexico/Tenochtitlan. European writers were eager to destroy all indigenous thought and traditions to justify the genocide of the indigenous nations.

As the Nahua traveled, they were always seeking similar places to duplicate their beloved Lake Mexico and Island of Aztlán and its similar surroundings. One of those locations was Mexcaltitlan, Nayarit whose ethnology is similar to the ancient Aztlán and its surroundings. Some historians mistake Mexcaltitlan for the original ancient Aztlán. Mexcaltitlan was just one of the many stops the Azteca/Mexica made on their long journey in search of the prophesized promise land, Mexico/Tenochtitlan. In addition, there is an island called San Pedro de Aztlán but it is right next to the Pacific Ocean.

The ancient tracks of the past can still be found in the hills, mountains, rocks and mesas that surround

the Lower Colorado River Valleys. Fortunately, they have escaped major destruction and now bear witness to the Mexica Creation Story on the Colorado River.

Huehuetlapallan on the Colorado River

Ill 46

Drawing from Orgullo de Aztlán. Un Reseña de Historia Mexicana by Esther R. Perez

Hueman wrote the "Divine Book" of the Tolteca. It narrates the history of the pilgrimage. Hueman guided the Tolteca from the red regions of Huehuetlapallan, the reddish Palen Mountain by the reddish Colorado River.

Ill 47

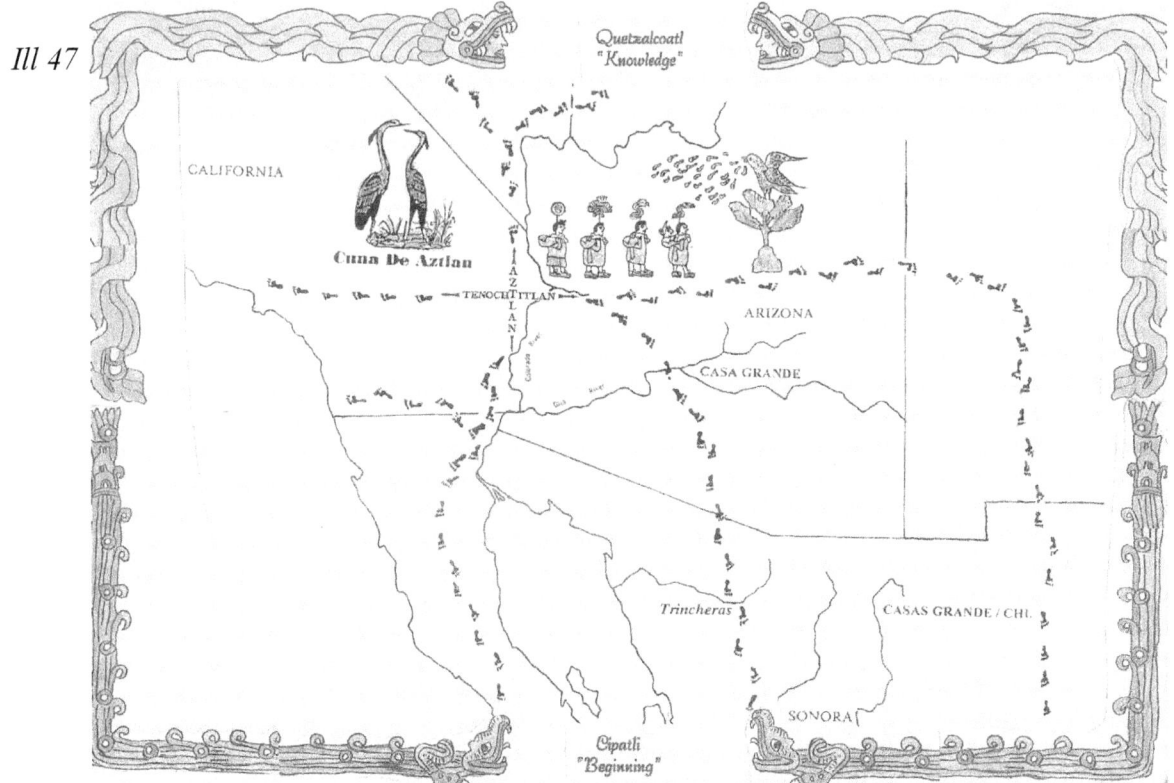

Migrations to the four directions center in the Palo Verde/Parker Valleys (Florencio Yescas & Alfredo A. Figueroa)

Boturini Codex, Fold 1 and 2

1. Calli (house), the different nations that left Aztlán at different times
2. The 52-year cycle of "El Fuego Nuevo" (the New Fire)
3. The Island of Aztlán
4. Teocalli, House of Worship
5. Chimalma, Mother of Quetzalcoatl. Her symbol is her shield beside her head
6. Ce-Acatl Quetzalcoatl
7. Man, on canoe crossing the Colorado River/Lake beginning the migration from Aztlán
8. Tecpatl (flint), Year one when they left Aztlán
9. Teoculhuacan (Twisted Peak) on the Big Maria Mountain Range
10. The Mexica would leave trails of footprints which are on the petroglyphs indication their migration.
11. Human face with the head of hummingbird in a cave is the symbol of Huitzilopochtli, the Father Sun urging the people to continue, Tihui,Tihui.
12. Xicomoztoc

Why Wasn't Aztlán Revealed Before?

The origin of Aztlán had not been revealed because the time had not arrived. The time is measured in the cosmos. The Mexica codices show how time was measured since time immemorial when a date synchronized on the lunar and solar calendars every 52 years during the rising of the Pleiades (Seven Sister Constellation) to its zenith at 12 midnight on November 14. The last 52-year New Year Fire Celebration occurred on November 14, 2003. (Star Date Magazine, University of Texas, November 14, 2003)

For the Mexica, the 52-year New Year fire celebration was the most important day of their lives. The passing of the Pleiades to its zenith at midnight marked a time of renewal of both the cosmos and on earth. This is when they celebrated the Binding of the 52-year ritual of the New Fire Ceremony.

The Mexica used two calendars. One marked the important cosmic events while the other kept a daily and seasons event. They believe that the world was reborn every time the calendars overlapped every 52 years. It marked the end of a phase in their lives and the renovation of a new one. This was called Xuihmolpilli, the binding of the years.

The lunar calendar marked 260 days and the solar calendar marked 365 solar days. After the passing of the Pleiades at midnight, and the world continued on its course, the Mexica celebrated the New Fire ceremony. The last New Fire ceremony celebrated by the Mexica, before the European invasion, was celebrated in 1483. 1483 was nine years before Columbus invaded Anahuac in 1492. The nine years represent the transition of ending of the 4th Sun to the beginning of the 5th Sun.

The day before the New Fire ceremony, all the fires in the valley were extinguished, household goods (ollas, cooking pots, metates, molcajetes) were broken and thrown away as a traditional ritual. Homes were swept clean. At dusk everyone would climb to the rooftops to wait for darkness, the commencement of the arriving of the Pleiades to its zenith from the east.

The celebration of the New Fire Ceremony took place at Cerro Estrella (Star Hill) in the suburb of Iztapalapa located southwest of downtown Mexico City. The hill is in the middle of the Valley of Anahuac. During the celebration, a huge fire was lit for this important event that could be seen for miles.

During the ceremony, the knowledge keepers (priests) would dress in ornaments that had the images of Huitzilopochtli, Tlaloc and Quetzalcoatl. As the sun began to set, they proceeded from the east, walking to the top of the teocalli (pyramid-shaped temple) located on top of Cerro Estrella. They would walk in solemn procession and in full observance pacing themselves with the travel of the Pleiades. The Mexica called them "Teonenemi" meaning they travel like the cosmic energies because they were emulating the rising of the Pleiades from the east to its zenith in the cosmos.

When the Pleiades were in the correct geometrical position and had passed its zenith at midnight the knowledge keepers knew the world would continue and they started the New Fire celebrations.

The priests lit four bundles, each with 52 sticks and runners would carry the lit torches from the ceremonial fire to the four directions and especially to El Templo Mayor in the Zocalo. The New Fire was ignited at Huitzilopochtli's Tlaloc teocalli (heart of the Mexica tradition and culture). This was the symbol of the beginning of a new life prompting a cry of relief and joy throughout Anahuac (Day, 1992)

The New Fire ceremony on earth was in conjunction with the cosmic counterpart to honor the Creator. The cosmic counterpart is the Leonid Meteor Showers. The Leonid Meteor Showers are seen every November 15 and have a unique role after the rising of the Pleiades which verifies the earth and cosmic archetype.

The rising of the Pleaides of November 14, 2003 was a very memorable and phenomenal event and was witnessed by Michelle Leivas Kristman, Demesia Figueroa and the author, Alfredo A. Figueroa. They were vigilant during that night from the patio of their house in the old neighborhood of Acacitli. They patiently watched the Pleiades travel to its zenith coming from the east continuing from sundown to midnight.

They had prepared themselves to observe this sacred event because early that morning they had heard the news on KERU Radio Bilingue program from Fresno, California. The program was from the McDonald's Observatory at the University of Texas and it mentioned that at midnight the Pleiades would rise to its zenith. This cosmic event confirmed that the starting anchor date for the 52-year cycle was not 1507 as previously believed. The news of the rising Pleiades took them completely by surprise because the majority of the Mexica investigators, historians anthropologists, including Don Salvador Juarez Rodriguez, 12th descendant of Cuauhtémoc, thought that the last 52-year New Fire celebration took place in 1507 before the European conquerors prohibited the celebration of the ceremony.

In the Colorado River Valleys, among the intaglios (geoglyphs) and petroglyphs are the symbols of the Pleiades (Boma Johnson).

The Pleiades petroglyphs are seen all along the paths of the migration that the indigenous took from Aztlán to the four directions. The glyph of the Pleiades near Gila Bend, Arizona is a well-known tourist attraction.

Continuing south to Sonora, Mexico of La Sierra Provedora, located 5 miles west of Caborca, there are hundreds of petroglyphs and there you will find the Pleiades images together with the Heron and turtle. The culmination of these three images signifies that the people came from the land of the Herons during the 52-year cycles that had left from Aztlán on the Colorado River.

In the surrounding areas of the Colorado River particularly in the Palo Verde Valley there are numerous archaeological sites that have an abundance of broken ollas, molcajetes and other household artifacts. These artifacts are semi-buried in the mesas along the valley alluding to the rituals of the New Fire ceremony.

Dr. Eloise Quinones Keber, author of the book, "Telleriano Remensis Codex," states the codex was completed in 1563, forty-two years after the Spanish Conquest.

Emmanuel Le Roy Ladurie, in his forward of the book, refers to the codex as one of the most remarkable 16th century Mexican colonial manuscript that is in the possession of the Bibliotheque Nationale: " *Indeed, its 50 pages of ivory-colored paper- whose beautiful watermarks indicate that it was probably manufactured in Genoa then shipped to Spain before reaching Mexico, then returned to Europe bound in to a book, could no longer tolerate the contact of hands, no matter how careful they might be. What is more, its deep colors, which render it so striking, could no longer endure being exposed to daylight without fading away.*"

As we read the forward, the codices went back and forth across the Atlantic Ocean and went through many hands before reading the library in France. In Folio 42r, you can see where the year of 1524 has been scratched out and the 1507 has been added.

The deception of the 1507 date was conceived by the European conquerors that included the Catholic Church who wanted to keep these sacred events from being known to the world. They deliberately distorted the date of 1483 to eliminate the Mexica's most important traditional ritual of the New Fire Ceremony that related to its cosmic duality.

This detrimental mathematical error is clearly depicted in the Telleriano-Remensis codex as it depicted the last New Fire ceremony had taken place in 1507.

The codex was painted during the Spanish Inquisition and is an excellent example of their devisive and malicious policy. The year 1507 has continued to be the date most of the modern-day archaeologists and historians have used as a starting (anchor) date that provides them with all the 52-year cycles leading up to the modern day New Year ceremonies celebrated annually during the month of March. The corrected cosmic mathematical calculation is based on the year 1483 as a starting (anchor) date and this is the last year the Mexica celebrated the New Fire Ceremony. The correct modern day ending anchor date of the New Fire Ceremony is November 14, 2003, based on the 52-year cycle correlated with the rising of the Pleiades, Seven Sister Constellation, to its zenith on November 14, 2003.

Telleriano-Remensis Codex
Erroneous Mathematical Measurement of Time

Ill 49

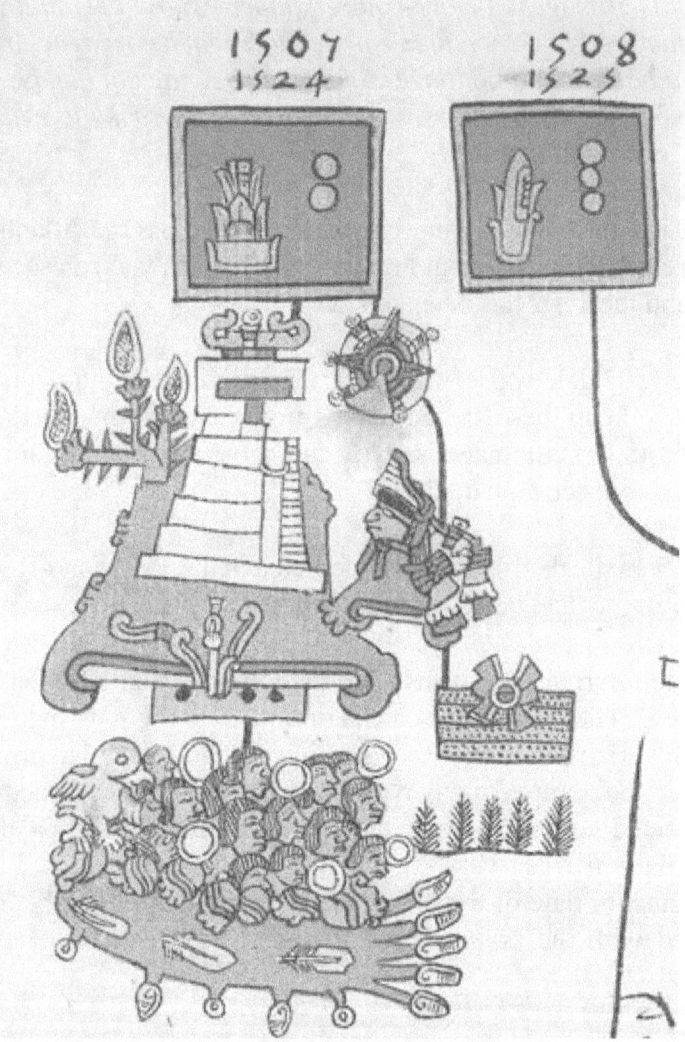

The Glyph from the Telleriano-Remensis codex, Folio 42V is depicting the New Fire ceremony that supposedly took place in 1507 marking out the year 1524 but both dates are incorrect. This was done purposely by the priests to destroy the native-cosmic tradition. This glyph was painted after the Spanish invasion. It was part of the notorious Catholic Church Spanish Inquisition. It was one of the worst devastations the indigenous people suffered in the Continent of Anahuac and to date, the brainwashing of our culture continues. If challenged, this document would never be accepted in a court of law. We know the last New Fire ceremony in Mexico was held in 1483. This is based on the 52-year cycle correlated with the rising of the Pleiades to its zenith on November 14, 2003.

52-Year Cycle Mathematical Breakdown

In the Mexica mathematical breakdown, 52-years form a cycle. Nine cycles multiplied by 52-years equals 468 years, which constitute one Mexica Sun.

The year 2003 was the beginning of the 9-year transition ending the 5th sun and the ending of the Era of Pisces on December 21, 2012.

There are Five Suns on the Aztec Sunstone Calendar. If we subtract 468 years from 2003, we get the year 1535, the last 52-year cycle and the year the Spaniards conquered most of Mexico. 1535 marked the end of the 4th Sun and the beginning of the 5th Sun. It brought the Sun of Darkness for the Indigenous people but for the conquering Europeans it was the New Sun of Light, because the conquerors sought to completely obliterate indigenous culture and traditions.

468 years multiplied by Five Suns equals 2340 years. Subtract 2340 years from 2003 and this date takes you back to the year 337 BC which was the beginning of the Era of Pisces. The Era of Pisces is characterized by the dominance of religion namely by the Jewish religion in the Middle East.

The Pisces zodiac image is symbolized by two fish. That is why they are shown in the Catholic religion also. These two fish of Pisces are in the geoglyphs at the Bouse Fisherman site that represents Tlaloc.

As we previously stated, the end of the Era of Pisces was also the end of the 5th Sun. We are now entering the 1st Sun of the Era of Ophiuchus, the 13th constellation. Its cosmic image is the blonde bearded man with a serpent wrapped around him that is the image of Quetzalcoatl in the cosmos. Every constellation has Five Suns as shown in the Aztec Sunstone calendar. To clarify, there are not six or seven Suns as many historians have stated.

The Five Suns of the Era of Pisces
9 Year Transition 2012 AD Beginning the First Sun of Ophiuchus

Ill 50

5th Sun	4th Sun	3rd Sun	2nd Sun	1st Sun
(9) 2003	(9) 1535	(9) 1067	(9) 599	(9) 131
− 52	− 52	− 52	− 52	− 52
----------	----------	----------	----------	----------
(8) 1951	(8) 1483	(8) 1015	(8) 547	(8) 79
− 52	− 52	− 52	− 52	− 52
----------	----------	----------	----------	----------
(7) 1899	(7) 1431	(7) 963	(7) 495	(7) 27AD
− 52	− 52	− 52	− 52	− 52
----------	----------	----------	----------	----------
(6) 1847	(6) 1379	(6) 911	(6) 443	(6) 25BC
− 52	− 52	− 52	− 52	+ 52
----------	----------	----------	----------	----------
(5) 1795	(5) 1327	(5) 859	(5) 391	(5) 77
− 52	− 52	− 52	− 52	+ 52
----------	----------	----------	----------	----------
(4) 1743	(4) 1275	(4) 807	(4) 339	(4) 129
− 52	− 52	− 52	− 52	+ 52
----------	----------	----------	----------	----------
(3) 1691	(3) 1223	(3) 755	(3) 287	(3) 181
− 52	− 52	− 52	− 52	+ 52
----------	----------	----------	----------	----------
(2) 1639	(2) 1171	(2) 703	(2) 235	(2) 233
− 52	− 52	− 52	− 52	+ 52
----------	----------	----------	----------	----------
(1) 1587	(1) 1119	(1) 651	(1) 183	(1) 285
− 52	− 52	− 52	− 52	+ 52
----------	----------	----------	----------	----------
1535	1067	599	131	337 BC
Defeat of Mexico	Mexica leave Aztlán	Fall of Tollan (Tula)	Teotihuacan began	

The Gregorian modern day calendar years are based on the birth of Jesus Christ. Before Jesus Christ was born is BC and after Jesus Christ was born is AD, Anno Domini, (In the year of our Lord). The indigenous calendar is based on the 52-year cycle and the cosmic rising of the Pleiades since time immemorial as shown on the Aztec Sunstone calendar.

Pleiades Seven Sisters Constellation
The Measurement of Time Since Time Immemorial

Ill 51

Ill 52

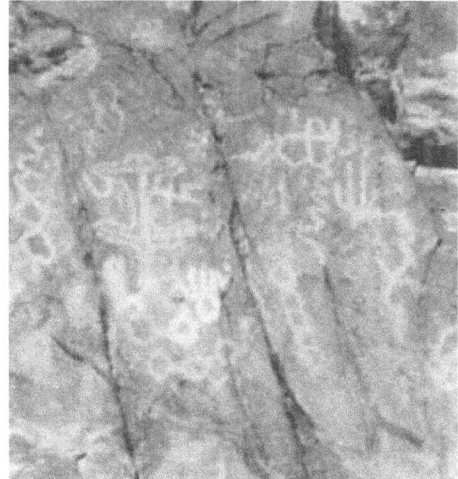

Petroglyph of the Pleiades Star Cluster at the base of the Tonantzin Peak in the Dome Rock Mountains. (Photo taken by Alfredo A. Figueroa)

Ill 53

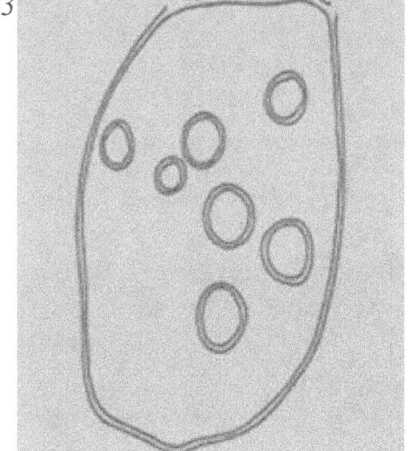

Pleiades Star Cluster Geoglyph Images at Blythe Giant Intaglios (Drawing from *Earth Figures of the Lower Colorado And Gila River Deserts: A Functional Analysis* by Boma Johnson)

52-Year Cycle
A Date on the Lunar and Solar Calendars

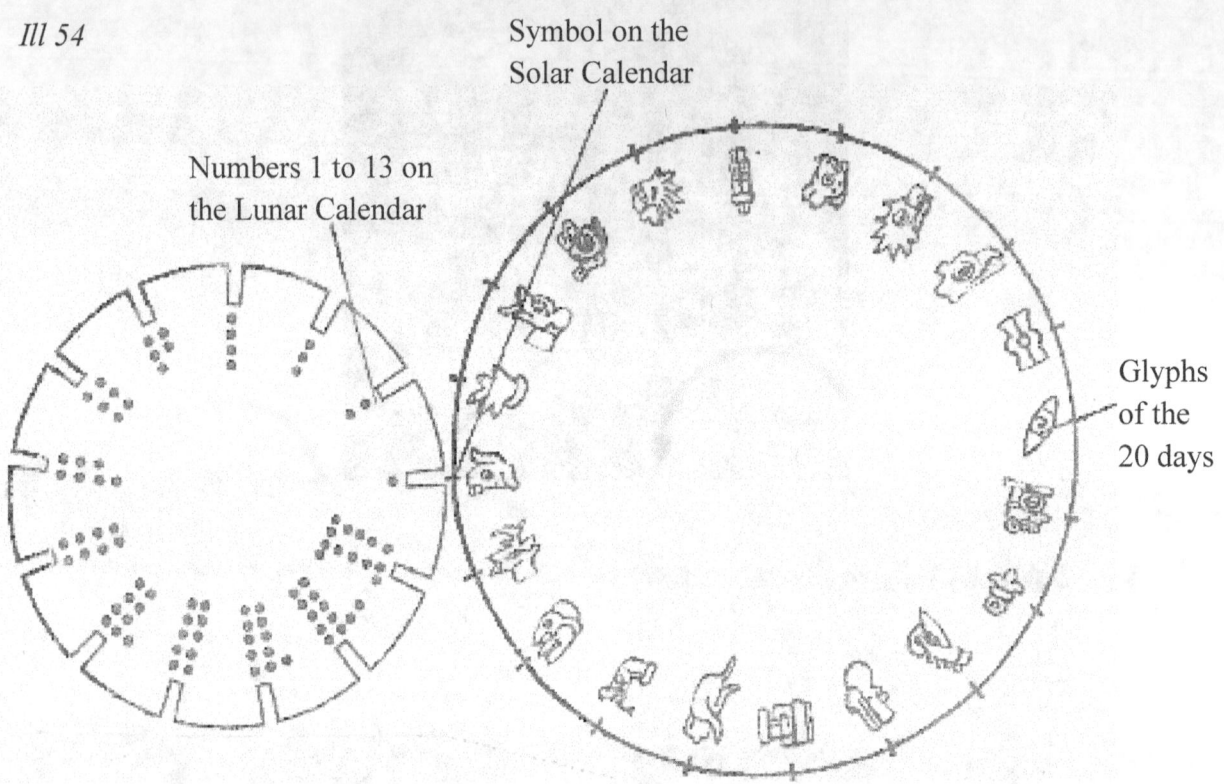

Ill 54

Numbers 1 to 13 on the Lunar Calendar

Symbol on the Solar Calendar

Glyphs of the 20 days

The renewal of a cycle is when a date in the Lunar and Solar calendars meet for the first time in 52 years which is the end of one cycle and the birth of a new one. This occurs when the Pleiades rise to its zenith. The Pleiades are called in Nahuatl, Tianquiztli, which means the marketplace, where all meet for their needs.

Huitzilopochtli and Its Relation to the Mexica New Fire Ceremony

Ill 55

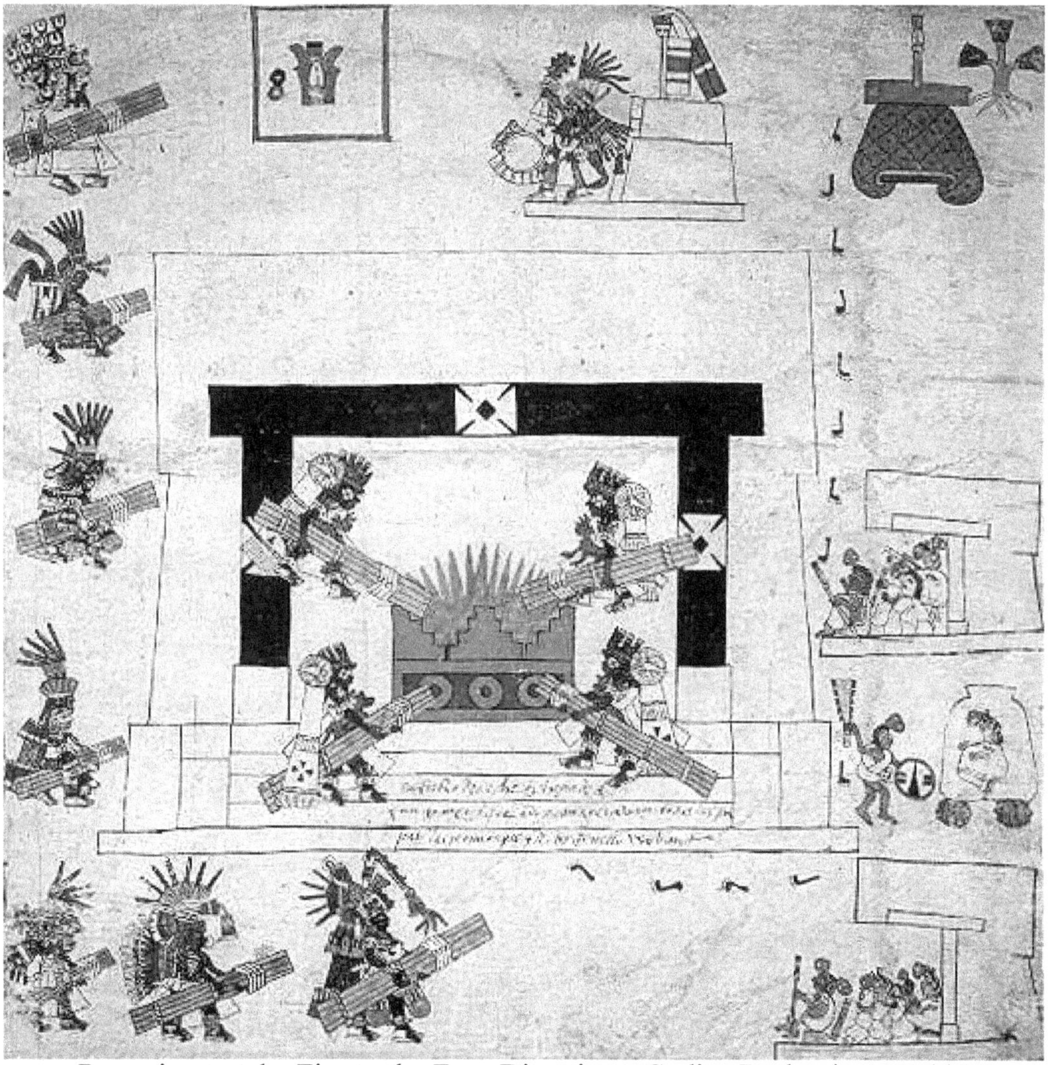

Preparing to take Fire to the Four Directions, Codice Borbonicus, Fold 34

November 14, the day before the Leonid Meteor Showers, is the rising of the Pleiades and the binding of the 52 years. They took the fire to the four directions. Even today, among our native relations, when you become 52 years old, you are given the title of Elder.

New Fire Ceremony at Cerro Estrella in Mexico City, Mexico

Ill 56

Upon the rising of the Pleiades to its zenith, the New Fire ceremony was celebrated all over Anahuac. (North American Continent). The New Fire ceremony was celebrated on earth as a duality to the Leonid meteor showers in the cosmos. During the 1992 Peace & Dignity Journey, organizers and runners were honored at Cerro Estrella by the City Council members of Mexico City with a New Fire Ceremony. It was one of the most spiritual and memorable occasions we have experienced. (Painting from the World of Moctezuma Aztec by Jane S. Day)

New Fire Ceremony-Florentine Codex

Ill 57

New Fire Ceremony in the Temples

Ill 58

Florentine Codex

Broken Pottery found at the base of the Mule Mountains in the Palo Verde Valley. (Photo taken by Alfredo Acosta Figueroa)

On the day of the rising of the Pleiades, all fires throughout Anahuac were extinguished. Household goods, cooking pots, metates and hearthstones were thrown away. All homes were swept clean inside and out. At dusk, everyone climbed to the rooftops to watch and wait for the rising of the Pleiades. When the Pleiades rose to its zenith at 12 midnight, the New Fire started (out with the old, in with the new). The is why remains of these types of artifacts can be found around the Palo Verde Valley.

Florencio Yescas

Ill 59

"Loor eterno en memoria a la voz reveladora en el desierto, enseñando y educando a los Xicanos con las danzas y del reencuentro con nuestra cultura, preparando el camino de la Nueva Sabiduría."

"Eternal remembrance and thanks to the memory of the voice that came to the desert, bringing forth education and teaching to all Xicanos, the danza and reencounter with our traditional culture that is preparing us for path of the New Knowledge." (Figueroa)   (Painting by Annika Lambert)

The first modern day Mexican historian of Mexica culture that came to California to retrace the Azteca/Mexica migration from Aztlán was Florencio Yescas, "El Gran Maestro" of La Danza Esplendor Azteca.

He was sent to the United States by Dr. Salvador Rodriguez from Ixcateopan, Guerrero, in the early 1970s to pave the way for the coming of Cuauhtémoc Spiritual Pilgrimage in 1985.

In the early 1970s, Yescas came to San Diego and Los Angeles, California and we met him for the first time in "El Centro Cultural" in San Diego. There we discussed and showed him our research. He offered his full cooperation and wanted to visit us in Blythe, California.

Yescas' overall mission was to teach the Danza Azteca to all the Xicanos in the United States. The danza is without exception one of the movements that has made a tremendous impact on the lives of Xicanos, who for years had been seeking the truth of the Mexica roots.

Yescas organized and informed Xicanos about the greatness of our indigenous traditions and culture. He also introduced them to the "Birth of the New Knowledge" (La Nueva Sabiduría) which is the revelation of Cuauhtémoc's Prophecy.

After touring the United States, Yescas finally visited the Palo Verde Valley to educate the community and prepare them for Cuauhtémoc's Spiritual Pilgrimage which was still in its planning stages. Yescas felt honored to visit Blythe. He told us that we should be very proud to live in the center of Aztlán. He referred to our indigenous culture in the lower Colorado River Valleys and of the Nahua migrations south to Mexico City. He cited the information from traditionalist oral history which stated that the Mexica came from Aztlán, a place along the Colorado River north of the confluence of the Colorado and Gila Rivers. Maestro Yescas urged the building of a cultural and educational center in Blythe because like us, he knew that this was indeed Aztlán.

Maestro Yescas was one of the most knowledgeable danzantes that memorialized the migration period of the Azteca/Mexica history through his danza. One of the oldest works performed by his danzantes honors the journey of the indigenous people from Aztlán which is called "La Migracion de Los Chichimeca" (The Chichimeca Migration).

Yescas was dedicated to his culture. He was one of the first Mexica historian who supported our research confirming that La Cuna de Aztlán was in the lower Colorado River Basin Valley. He knew that his time was limited to fulfill his commitment to Dr. Salvador Rodriguez, the 12th descendent of Cuauhtémoc to prepare the Cuauhtémoc Spiritual Pilgrimage that was forthcoming.

Florencio Yescas' journey to this country fulfilled part of the prophecies stated in Cuauhtémoc's decree on August 13, 1521 which briefly states,

> "Our Sun has gone from our vision and we will soon be in the dark but the time will come when our Sun will shine again. Then we will again build our schools (calmekas) and cultural centers (Kuiakaltin) of danza and song, and demanding justice and equality."

Florencio Yescas' return to Aztlán was the last leg of his journey on the Road to Aztlán, fully completing the circle of the Mexica migration.

The Mexica migration that had once left Aztlán on the Colorado River in 1067 was now returning to break ground for the Cuauhtémoc Spiritual Pilgrimage that was coming from Ixcateopan, Guerrero, Mexico.

Cuauhtemoc's Spiritual March
Return to Aztlán

Ill 60

Dr. Salvador Rodriguez giving instructions and final blessings to Estrella Newman and Hunbatz Men while Don Salvador's daughter, Maria Alberta del Olmo, look on at the beginning of the Cuauhtémoc Spiritual March in December 1985 in Ixcateopan, Guerrero. (Photo by Darline Burns)

According to Cuauhtémoc's descendants, the revelation of the location of Cuauhtémoc's tomb in Ixcateopan, Guerrero was a sign that the age of darkness was ending.

Cuauhtémoc's 12th descendant, Dr. Salvador Rodriguez was aging and his life was coming to an end. He could no longer see and was in poor health. Still, he was determined to continue and fulfill Cuauhtémoc's prophecy, "that our sun would shine again." Therefore, he ordered the revival of "La Ceremonia de Fuego Nuevo (The New Fire Ceremony)."

The New Fire Ceremony initialed the Cuauhtémoc Spiritual Pilgrimage that was going to end on Cuauhtémoc's birthday on February 23, 1986 in Los Angeles, California.

The director of Mexico City's Taller Escuela Julian Carillo, Estrella Newman, leader of the Mexicanidad Movement and Hunbatz Men, Mayan traditional leader, were chosen to organize the journey that would bring the "Sacred Fire" (the lighted torch) from the tomb of Cuauhtemoc back to

Aztlán on the Colorado River.

Dr. Rodriguez gave his final blessing to the participants of the Cuauhtémoc Spiritual Pilgrimage in Ixcateopan, Guerrero. He lit the eternal torch on December 7, 1985 at the end of the New Fire Ceremony. The Sacred Fire would arrive in Los Angeles on Cuauhtémoc's birthday, February 23. The pilgrimage was composed of native traditionalists and people of various religions and faiths. Among them was a Buddhist monk from Japan who was inspired by the similarity between his beliefs and those of the Nahua.

After the participants left Ixcateopan, they arrived in El Zocalo in Mexico City where they were greeted by thousands of school children and a large group of danzantes as well as the president of the Universidad Nacional Autonoma de Mexico, Dr. Jorge Carpizo who gave them the official welcome. Together they participated in "La Ceremonia del Fuego Nuevo". The participants then continued to the Teocalli del Sol in Teotihuacan, where the ancient rites were performed in their honor on top of the Teocalli del Sol (Pyramid of the Sun).

The historical journey continued north to Cuidad Juarez, Chihuahua. In El Paso, Texas, however, the participants clashed with modern reality. They were unable to cross the border like their forefathers, the Azteca/Mexica had hundreds of years before. They were required to present a visa or post a $1,000 bond to be able to cross the International border created by the United States in 1848. This was a traumatizing reminder of the changes that had taken place over the past century when indigenous people were free to traverse throughout the continent.

After crossing the artificial border that bifurcates indigenous blood heritage from its place of origin, the few participants who were able to post bond imposed by the United States Immigration to cross over to the United States took the message of Cuauhtémoc to a number reservations in the southwest, among them the Hopi, Pueblo and Navajo. (Hunbatz Men)

When the participants finally arrived at Parker, Arizona, they were greeted by the Elders as they arrived at the Colorado River Indian Tribes Reservation (CRIT). This meeting became more fulfilling by the realization that they had reached the ancient Island of Aztlán. This was a joyful event that included the singing of bird songs, which stipulate the migration of the natives from Aztlán to the four directions that took place for thousands of years. The participants of the pilgrimage were bringing to fruition the oral history of what speaks of the descendants of Moctezuma and Cuauhtémoc returning to Mexico/Aztlán, their place of origin. (Gilbert Leivas)

Cuauhtémoc's parents were descendants of the lower Colorado River area. His mother was Chontal (members of the Hokan linguistic family that includes the Mojave, Cocopah and Quechan). His father was Mexica (members of the Uto-Aztecan linguistic family that includes the Chemehuevi and Hopi).

The next stop of the pilgrimage was La Escuela de la Raza Unida (ERU) in Blythe, California. At la Escuela, a large crowd gathered to welcome the group. Although we did not know of Dr. Salvador Rodriguez, he knew about us and this was made evident because when the participants arrived at ERU,

Hunbatz Men said, "We are looking for the people of Aztlán and we are bringing them greetings from the descendant of Cuauhtémoc." The crowd at ERU was overwhelmed when they realized that their school was known in Southern Mexico.

During their brief time in Blythe, the pilgrimage participants gave informative lectures about Cuauhtémoc prophecies, explaining the significance of the pilgrimage and the history of the New Fire Ceremony. At the same time, the Sacred New Fire rituals were performed.

Upon leaving to continue the pilgrimage, Hunbatz Men invited ERU students and personnel from Blythe to join the group at Lincoln park in Los Angeles, to participate in Cuauhtémoc's birthday celebration on February 23, 1986. La Escuela took a large group of students and personnel to participate in the event in Los Angeles. It was a joyful event, where over 500 danzantes and "matachines" performed danzas and other traditional ceremonies.

During the final celebration of the pilgrimage at Lincoln Park, Chief Manuel Rocha (now deceased) of the Gabrileños of Los Angeles and Chief Victor "Sky Eagle" Lopez (now deceased) of the Chumash addressed the audience. Chief Lopez told the crowd, "Cuauhtémoc to the indigenous people represented George Washington and Abraham Lincoln all rolled into one." The Los Angeles celebration permeated with spirit, pride and joy. The centuries-old quest to return to Aztlán was completed. Cortes may have killed Cuauhtémoc in 1525 but his spirit will continue to live forever in the minds and spirits of the Xicano/indigenous people.

After Cuauhtémoc's Spiritual Pilgrimage in Los Angeles, Hunbatz Men and Felipe Villanueva went with the author to visit the Blythe Giant Intaglios and other sacred sites in the Palo Verde/Parker Valleys.

Many blessings resulted from the 1985 Cuauhtémoc Spiritual Pilgrimage. Besides returning the Sacred Fire to Aztlán, ties were established with the descendants of Cuauhtémoc in Ixcateopan, Guerrero. After the Pilgrimage, correspondence was received from Dr. Salvador Rodriguez Juarez, inviting us to visit Ixcateopan and the tomb of Cuauhtémoc.

Ill 61

Colorado River Indian Tribes Elders Helen Swick and John Soto receiving and welcoming the Cuauhtémoc Pilgrimage at the Tribal Administration

Finally, in December 1990, the group from Blythe visited Dr. Rodriguez thus fulfilling the cycle of "Desde la Cuna de Aztlán hasta la Tumba de Cuauhtémoc" (from the Cradle of Aztlán to the Tomb of Cuauhtémoc).

Conclusion

We have cross-referenced the origin of Aztlán with a copy of the original Mexico/United States Treaty of Guadalupe map that ended the war with Mexico on February 2, 1848 and with the numerous of Mexica codices, Blythe Giant Intaglios plus geoglyphs, petroglyphs, pictographs, lower Colorado River Basin Valleys surrounding mountains, native oral history, names and images, Nahuatl language of the sacred sites plus the crucial evidence of the sacred spring equinox cosmic event. The ancient tracks of the past thousands of years can still be found in the rocks, mountains and mesetas around the Palo Verde/Parker Valleys. Fortunately, they have escaped major destruction and now bear witness to the Mexica Creation Story on the Colorado River. All these evidentiary facts leave very little doubt of the origin of the mystical Island of Aztlán.

Pan-Che-Bek
"Seek the Roots of the Truth"

Why Don't We Know the Truth in the United States

Ill 62

Tlamantini (Mexica Teacher) teaching the new generation at the Calmeca (college) about the Creation Story using the codices.

We have never been taught about our true meaning on earth and why we as humans are the guardians of Mother Earth and that it is our mission to promote a harmonious equilibrium among all species.

Tres Cientificos Mexicanos by Ignacio Bernal

The following is a translation that I took from the book, *Tres Cientificos Mexicanos* by Ignacio Bernal. Though I never him in person, we did have long conversations on the phone when he was visiting Rio Hondo College in the 1980s. Ignacio Bernal and Alfonso Caso are two of the most renowned investigators of the Aztec culture. They are both now deceased.

This translation is of Bernal's thoughts when writing about the Aztec calendar's correlation to the Aztec years and the Christian years.

"One of the major difficulties that the investigator who tries to study the ancient Aztec civilization stumbles over is his own manner of thinking. This is determined by his European education that runs constantly the risk of admitting the evidence that is just the result of one's customs and rejects as impossible those solutions that are repugnant with his particular mode of seeing and resolving a problem.

Maybe because in the concrete mind, the logical and the illogical mix. Maybe, also because our habits of thinking, individually or collectively, are taken unconsciously like universal rules of thinking. The truth is the task that is more difficult for the ethnologist and the archaeologists, is to translate European thought to other ways of thinking. Even looking paradoxical, we have to understand other spirits, prescinding to a certain point, our own spirit.

The methodological mistake reached a point that many investigators do not agree to admit that their own system was the one that the Indigenous had utilized in forming the calendar. Instead they express their arrogance even criticize for not having realized some of the most wonderful combinations without considering that maybe the Natives didn't have the same intentions that they had.

In proposing to study the Aztec calendar and its correlation to the Christian calendar... I have tried to abandon up to where it's been possible the prejudice European thinking, which I myself have incurred and I have studied the problem of how this calendar as the Aztec understood it and not to think in accord with the idea of a European astronomer.

I consider that the inscriptions on the rocks are the most genuine source of knowledge in the manner of the thinking of the ancient Natives. Likewise, are the paintings which in reality, are very few, that have been discovered on the monument. In both cases, they are absolutely authentic data that show the thinking of the Indigenous. You can incur an error by the wrong interpretation of the inscriptions or because the scribe was mistaken."

What Will Happen After 2012?

Many people were concerned and worried about what would happen after 2012. They based their concerns on what was the global interest in the Maya "doom day prophecy". Accordingly, to the representatives of the indigenous people, the apocalyptic forecast was misunderstood. December 21, 2012 marked the end of the grand cycle of 13-144,000 days, Baktuns, lasting 5126 years coinciding with the winter solstice in the Northern Hemisphere. The Mayan historians said the long count will start again. The world will not end but a new era will begin.

This is the same thing that many people asked for many years, "What is going to happen after December 21, 2012?" All we can respond is what happened after the end of the 4th Sun in 1535 when the Spanish invaders conquered most of Anahuac killing millions of natives. Never in the world history up to that time had a conquered nation been so brutally obliterated leaving few natives alive, committing the atrocity of genocide.

In Europe, when the conquerors won a war, they would just kill the kings and move into their castle. This is why there are so many well-preserved castles in different countries all over Europe. On the contrary, in the invasion of Mexico, Tenochtitlan, one of the first structures to be destroyed was the twin towers of Huitzilopochtli/Tlaloc in the Plaza Mayor in the center of Mexico/Tenochtitlan. It was destroyed together with the sacred images because it represented the power of the Confederation of the Anahuac that extended all the way from the Rocky Mountains of Montana down to Nicaragua. Something similar occurred in New York City when the twin towers were destroyed on September 11, 2001. They represented the World Trade Center that represented the central capitalist power of the world. So, what is going to happen? You must analyze what happened before when humans forgot their roles on earth and sought their own self-interest.

We are taught to have faith and hope in tough times but the world is so corrupt and very few people are pursuing their obligations to maintain a harmonious equilibrium on earth. The Era of Ophiuchus, the 13th constellation is the return of Quetzalcoatl, the 13th level of knowledge. Its cosmic image is a snake wrapped around a blonde bearded man. We must revert to cosmic cultural archetype tradition as a people and as guardians of Mother Earth. We will not get there by the imposition of human self-interest decree that has brought us to this stage of crisis. Humans must realize their obligations of global preservation and conservation.

Re-Encounter with
Our Spiritual and Cultural Ancestral Roots

Ill 63

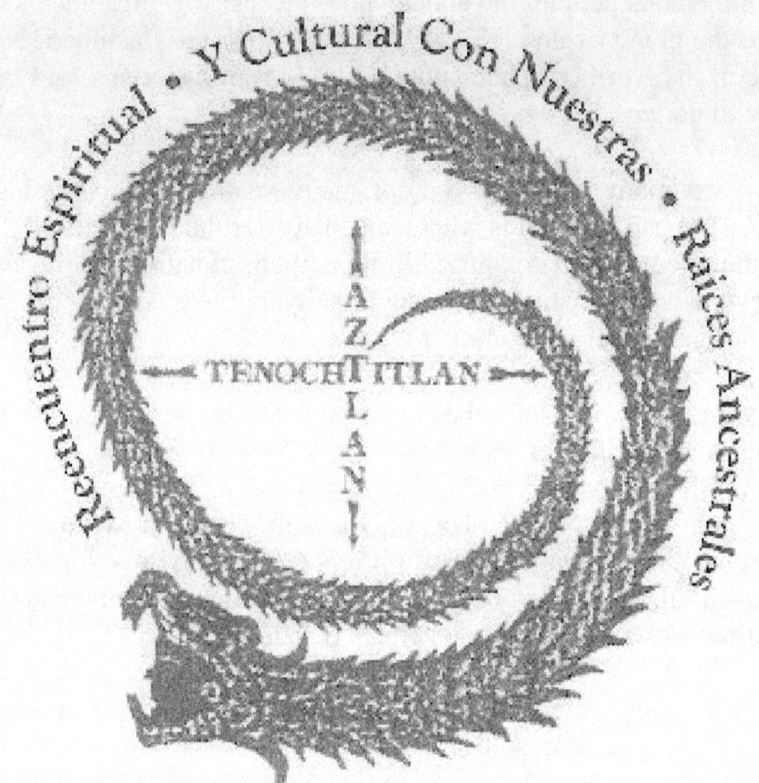

Alfredo A. Figueroa & Florencio Yescas

What can we do to regain our mission on earth? We do not use the word hope or faith but rather we are able to present facts and that is what we need to pursue.

Unless we reject our human selfish greed and combine our efforts to preserve Mother Earth, our spiritual, cultural and cosmic traditions will disappear. Capitalism is the direct opposite of indigenous cultural cosmic tradition.

"The vision of our past greatness and catastrophe that happened upon our country since the Cortes invasion up to this date should stimulate us to recover the residues left over of this collapse. To save the indigenous culture is to save ourselves and reconstruct our greatness, Tihui, Tihui" (Los Gobiernos Socialistas de Anahuac, Dr. Ignacio Romervargas Yurbide, 1978)

Nahuatl Prophecy

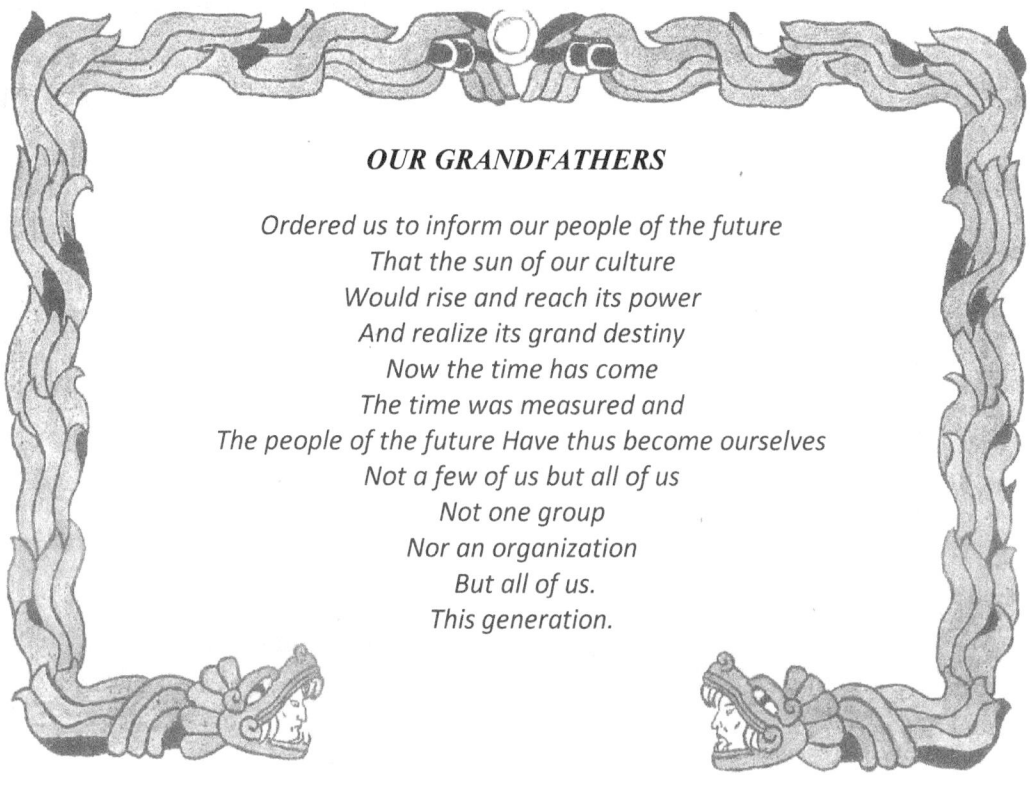

OUR GRANDFATHERS

*Ordered us to inform our people of the future
That the sun of our culture
Would rise and reach its power
And realize its grand destiny
Now the time has come
The time was measured and
The people of the future Have thus become ourselves
Not a few of us but all of us
Not one group
Nor an organization
But all of us.
This generation.*

When the petroglyphic monoliths rise by themselves, then the time has come to tell the truth and the New Sun will shine upon us and will speak the greatness of the Mexica.

***As long as the world will endure, the fame and glory of Mexico/Tenochtitlan will never perish.**excellent

Biography of Alfredo Acosta Figueroa

Alfredo Acosta Figueroa was born in Blythe, California in 1934. He is the fourth son of a 5th-generation family of indigenous-Xicano heritage from the Colorado River Indian Reservation which encompasses the Palo Verde/Parker Valleys.

Alfredo's family was the only existing family that began mining during the famous La Paz, Arizona-Colorado River Gold Rush in 1862. He retired in 2006.

Alfredo's mother, Carmen Acosta Figueroa was a long-time midwife and volunteer social worker and was well known for her resourcefulness and generosity to the community like what her mother, Dolores Mollinedo was on the reservation.

His father, Danuario Gomez Figueroa was of Yaqui-Pima descent from San Jose de Pima, Sonora, Mexico. He instilled in his sons a strong independent virtue as self-employed miners and he would say, "Your boss is your biggest enemy." He believed that we should share with others and that the biggest crime one could commit was to deny workers a just wage.

Alfredo credits his mother, father and siblings for his healthy and strong upbringing as a youth and this has been the fundamental base of his family. He and his siblings grew up in "El Barrio del Cuchillo", a neighborhood in Blythe referred by Chemehuevi elders as "El Barrio del la Liebre," and it Nahuatl, it is the ancient "Acacitli."

Alfredo and his wife, Demesia have been blessed with 9 children, 26 grandchildren, 27 great-grandchildren and 1 great-great-grandchild. All are the corner stone of his multiple activities.

In the late 1950s, Alfredo and his brothers became actively involved in politics in Blythe. During this time, Blythe was known as "the Little Mississippi" because of the rampant racial discrimination by the Anglo-dominated power brokers against Xicanos and other minorities. The Figueroa brothers fought against civil injustices in Blythe and throughout California.

He has worn many hats and undertaken numerous roles including that of a "gambusino" (miner) all his life, civil rights activist, humanitarian, farm labor organizer (UFW), staunch environmentalist, anti-nuclear activist, historian, political coordinator, boxing coordinator, folkloric singer and guitarist and indigenous traditionalist.

His fascination with his indigenous heritage, birthplace and the geographic surroundings in the lower Colorado River Basin Valleys and Northwest Sonora, Mexico have been the main focus of his interests and accomplishments.

He was fortunate to have served for many years under the personal leadership of two highly respected Xicano leaders, Humberto "Bert" Corona of the Mexican American Political Association (MAPA) and Cesar Estrada Chavez, United Farm Workers (UFW). His experiences with Corona and Chavez deepened his esteem for humanity and encouraged him to pursue his goals.

Alfredo's involvement in the farm worker movement began in 1960. He first joined the Agricultural Workers Organizing Committee (AFL-CIO/AWOC) lettuce strike in the Imperial Valley as a volunteer organizer.

In 1963, Alfredo's life changed forever when he was brutally beaten by a couple of Anglo police officers. Alfredo was arrested and beaten inside a local restaurant, "El Sarape". After winning his case in the Justice of the Peace Court in Blythe, his family then sued the police officers and the City of Blythe. Finally, after 4 years, on April 17, 1967, he won his suit in Superior Court in Indio.

His case became a "cause célébre" in the Civil Rights Movement because he was one of the first Xicanos to sue City Hall and the police department and win in the State of California. His case appeared in the 1970 publication of <u>Mexican Americans and the Administration of Justice in the Southwest</u>, a report issued by the United States Civil Rights Commission. (Washington D.C. March 1970)

In 1962, Cesar Estrada Chavez started organizing the United Farm Workers Association (UFWA) which later became known as the United Farm Workers, AFL-CIO. In 1966, Alfredo once more became involved in organizing campesinos to fight for their rights and need for a union to protect them.

During the early years of the Coachella grape strike, he was involved in what was publicized as the Coachella Four Clap-Down Case. Alfredo was arrested and incarcerated with three other men, Raul Loya, Thomas Patrick Kay and Jim Caswell. They were accused of disrupting a public assembly when Alfredo lifted the United Farm Worker flag during a Fourth of July 1968 celebration at the Dateland school field in Coachella and the crowd cried out in unison "Huelga, Huelga, Huelga." This case was appealed all the way to the California Supreme Court and won after one of the defendants, Jim Caswell, died because of lack of medical attention after serving 52 of a 120-day sentence in the Riverside County jail.

The Cough Syrup case of 1969 is another incident that involved the physical abuse and unjustified incarceration of Alfredo and his brother, Gilbert by U.S. Customs officers. It occurred in Calexico, Ca at the border crossing. The case was heard in the 9th U.S. District Federal Court of San Diego, Ca and they were released.

Alfredo and Gilbert sued the Customs officers in the case of Figueroa v. Donald Quick. The presiding federal judge, Clifford Wallace issued a historical memorandum opinion that stated, "any violation of the Fourth Amendment could not be considered within the score of the official duties of an officer of the government and therefore he has no immunity of such acts." Prior t this case, Customs and Border Patrol Officers of the U.S. Department of Treasury had always been immune to lawsuits. This case set precedent giving victims abused by Customs and Border Patrol Officers the right to sue the U.S. Department of Treasury.

On April 6, 1972, Alfredo's daughter, Patricia was manhandled by the principal of Blythe Junior High School. They were having a "MECHA" (Xicano Student Organization) meeting and were showing an 8mm video where the United Farm Workers were protesting against former U.S. President Richard Nixon at the Los Angeles Convention Center. The Blythe Junior High principal, Earl Trout came in and became upset because two high school students were showing this movie in the meeting. He then disconnected the movie camera, grabbed Patricia and threw her out the door where she landed on her shoulders causing her injuries.

There were over 70 young Xicano students present who became enraged. This led to the four-week boycott of the high school and junior high. After seeing that the principal had not been reprimanded, the students and parents decided to start their own school at the city park. Thus, La Escuela de la Raza Unida officially began on May 1, 1972 under the famous phrase, "*<u>A la sombra de un arbol, una aula escolar, asi a los cuatro vientos</u>" <u>(a classroom under the shade of every tree, to the four winds).</u>*

In 1975, Alfredo and his family represented Xicanos at the Smithsonian Folk Life celebration in Washington D.C. In 1976, he was again invited during the Bicentennial celebrations.

Alfredo was the driving force in starting their own Bilingual Educational Radio station, KERU (88.5 FM) in 1982. It is now affiliated with Radio Bilingue from Fresno, California.

Under the leadership of Alfredo in 1976, ERU was instrumental in organizing local residents, Riverside County Cahuilla Tribes and Mexico to oppose the proposed Sun Desert Nuclear power plant of the San Diego Gas and Electric Company (SDG&E). It was to be built 15 miles southwest of Blythe at the base of the sacred Mule Mountains (Calli). SDG&E purchased 10,000 acres to obtain the water rights to supply the proposed Nuclear Power Plant displacing hundreds of local farm workers of the John Norton Farms. This plant posed a major threat to the contamination of the Lower Colorado River. They were successful in stopping the construction of the proposed Nuclear Power Plant. It was the first plant in the United States that was stopped.

In 1985, Alfredo and his brother Miguel were instrumental in lobbying for the construction of the Chuckwalla State Prison located 17 miles from Blythe.

Continuing with the anti-nuclear campaign in 1992, Ron Van Fleet and Alfredo, under the auspices of Fort Mojave Nation, organized the Colorado River Anti-Ward Valley Coordinating Committee. This committee was organized to stop the proposed construction of the Ward Valley Nuclear Toxic dump. The dump was proposed to be built 20 miles west of Needles and it was going to contaminate the aquifers that lead to the Colorado River. They were successful in getting the five Indigenous Reservations of the Colorado River to come together to fight the proposed dump. After struggling for 8-years together with the help of over 200 environmental organizations in the United States and Mexico, they stopped the construction of the proposed Ward Valley Nuclear Toxic Dump.

In 1992, he was the coordinator for the Colorado River Area Peace and Dignity Journeys that began in Alaska and Tierra del Fuego, South America. These journeys began simultaneously and ended in

Teotihuacan, Mexico on October 12, 1992 (Commemorating 500 years of European resistance) and again in 1996.

In 2000, together with the Indigenous communities of the Lower Colorado River Basin and environmentalist groups, they managed to detour the north route of the proposed PG&E Natural Gas Company line route (which went from Blythe, south to Baja California, Mexico). The proposed route threatened to destroy some of the most sacred sites of Palo Verde Peak. Thanks to their efforts, the sacred sites were preserved. Alfredo's traditional spirituality and his faith in the Creator have given him the motivation to pursue his goals and to seek the knowledge in revealing the truth of the creation story.

Throughout his life, he has received many recognitions and awards. He was the recipient of the prestigious Taller Escuela Julian Carrillo Honorary Award for his cultural investigations of Aztlán. He is also a descendant/ founder and president of the International Association of the Descendants of Joaquin Murrieta which was founded in 1988. He was co-organizer of the annual "Caravana Del Recuerdo" celebrations in Trincheras, Sonora (birthplace of Joaquin Murrieta) from 1988-2002.

Alfredo is a founding member of La Cuna de Aztlán Sacred Sites Protection Circle that signed a Memorandum of Understanding (MOU) with the Bureau of Land Management (BLM) to preserve the Blythe Giant Intaglios and over 300 sacred sites, on March 14, 2008.

Currently the Indigenous Tribes and Environmental Organizations along with Environmentalists are fighting one of the biggest struggles of their lives. They are fighting to protect the giant Kokopilli, Cicimitl, El Tosco geoglyph group and other sacred sites on the verge of being destroyed by the construction of the mega-solar power plants funded by government fast-track stimulus monies.

Despite the enormous obstacles that he has encountered throughout his life, Alfredo is not one that will give up. His long-life desire is to share, educate, and organize and regain the Indigenous Cosmic Traditional Culture which is the only solution for human salvation. One of his famous sayings is "La Lucha Indeterminable," (The Never-Ending Struggle). The compelling force behind Alfredo has been his strong dedication and the persistence in the belief of "El Nuevo Saber," The Birth of the New Knowledge, the Neltiliztli, meaning "to seek the roots of the truth without a shadow of a doubt."

Alfredo's philosophy is that all humans must come together as a family; Anglo-Saxons, Blacks, Indigenous and Asians, etc., like the ancient Nahuatl teachings of 'Tloque Nahuaque,' which is represented by the fingers on the hand, separate, different sizes and shapes, yet joined all together at the wrist as the human race, symbolizing, "that among all we do all for the benefits of all."

Ill 64

Alfredo Acosta Figueroa with the geoglyph image of Cicimitl as shown in the Los Angeles Times article title *"Near Blythe, Historian sees Solar Plants as threats of Desert carvings"*, April 24, 2010.

Nahuatl/Mexica Glossary

ACACITLI: A-atl-water, Ca-calli-house, Citli-Jackrabbit. "Jackrabbit in his house in the tulles;" the original name of Blythe, Barrio de la Liebre

ANAHUAC: The original Nahuatl name of today's North American Continent

A TLA CHINOLLI: A-atl-Water, Tla- tlalli-Earth, Chinolli-Fire "Water, Earth and Fire." geoglyph located at the Blythe Giant Intaglio/Ometecuhtli group.

ATOTONILCO: A-atl-Water, Toto-Hot, Nil-nilli-Within, Co-Place Place of the thermal water, "agua caliente."

AZCALLI: alabaster, whitish variety of gypsum, from the word Aztlán

AZCATITLAN CODEX: Fold #12 glyph of a baby in a cradle and the mother beside it, represents the base of the White Limestone Tunderbird Eagle that is in the form of an oblong bowl, thus the name "Cradle of Aztlán"

AZTAPILTIC: land of the whiteness, refers to Aztlán

AZTATL: Blue Heron, symbol of Aztlán

AZTECA: (plural) interchangeable with Mexica; associated with today's Xicano/Mexica; given the name because they were the first to come from Aztlán.

AZTECATL: (singular)Azt-Aztlán, Tecatl-Person; Person from Aztlan

AZTLÁN: Azt-Aztl-Heron, Tlan Place; Land of the Heron, Land of Whiteness, Land of the First Sunrise; Origin of the Nahua nations where civilization began on the Colorado River.

AZTLI: Wing

CALLI: Earth/House; One of the Four Astros on the Aztec Sunstone Calendar; represents earth, Mule Mountains, 15 miles southwest of Blythe

CALMECA: Cal-CAlli-House, Meca-mecate-measurement; Long house, the Mexica institution of higher learning (Sahagun)

CALPULLI: Barrio, suburb, social institution, similar to a native clan. The form of government that was used by the Mexica based on a highly socialistic form of equalitiy.

CHICANO: See Xicano

CHIMALHUACAN: Chimal-Chimalli-Shield, Hua-possesive, Can-place; Place of the shield, big white limestone mountain image of shield on the side of the Big Maria Mountains.

CHIMALLI: Shield

CHIMALMA: Chimal-Chimalli-Shield, Ma-embedded, Place of the Embedded Shield; another name for Cihuatlcoatl

CIHUATLCOATL: Cihuat-Cihuatl-Woman, Coatl-Snake; Snake Woman

CITLALTEPETL: Citlal-Citlalin-Star, Tepetl-Mountain; "Cerro Estrella" located at Iztapalapa, suburb of Mexico Cuity where the

52-year New Fire Ceremony took place.

CITLI: Jackrabbit

COATEPETL: Coat-Coatl-Snake, Tepetl-Mountain; Snake Mountain (Big Maria Mountains)

CODEX: Original manuscript painted glyphs; painted on Amatl (bark paper) by the Mexica "Tlacuillo" artist

CONFEDERATION OF ANAHUAC: All the nations that belonged to the Confederation from the Shoshone on the Rocky Mountains in the north down to Nicaragua in the south

CUAUHTEMOC: Cuauh-Cuauhtli-Eagle, Temoc-Descend; "Eagle that Descends"; symbolizes the Nahualli of the descending Sun; manifested on Eagle Mountain during the summer solstice; the 11th Tlatoani

EHECATL: Wind, Morning Star, twin of Xolotl the dog (evening star); Nahualli is the Gila woodpecker; Venus represents Ehecatl, Xolotl and Quetzalcoatl

HUEHUETEOTL: Hue-Ancient, Hue-Ancient, Teotl-Energy, Old image of the Creator

HUEHUETLAPALLAN: Hue-Ancient, Hue-Ancient, Tla-Tlalli-Earth; Pallan-Red Tinged; "Place of the Ancient-Ancient Red Tinged Earth"; Palen Mountain

HUEMAN: Gran Señor of the Toltecas who wrote the Divine Book and guided them on their migration south from the red regions of Huehuetlapallan in the Colorado River Valleys.

HUITZILOPOCHTLI: Huitzil-Huitzilin-Hummingbird, Opochtli-Left handed; the Left-handed Hummingbird" The humminbird is the nahualli of the Sun at 12 noon when it is at its zenith during the day and during the summer soltice it is the longest day of the year. During the solstice 6/21, daylight is the same for 4 days.

IPALNEMOHUANI: The Creator; "He who has no name, yet has all names"; the giver of life and all that exists whom we live for, symbolized by the "Divne Eye" image in the middle peak of the Mule Muntains and the northern point of the Omeyocan Diamond.

IXCATEOPAN: "The Altar of the Mexican Nation" and the "Birth of the New Knowledge"; Modified from Izcatemoteopan; A town in the State of Guerrero, Mexico where Cuauhtemoc was born and his remains are located.

MECITLI: Me-Metzli-Moon, Citli-Jackrabbit; "Jackrabbit in the Moon" The Creator's image that descends from the cosmos at Tamoanchan (Granite Peak); the one who changed the Azteca name to Mexica when they left the Colorado River at the end of the 3rd Sun. People in Mexico are called Mexica in honor of Mecitli, the Creator.

METZLIAPAN: Metzli-Moon, Apan-Lake, Moon Lake

MEXICO: Me-Metzli-Moon, Xi-Xichtl-Umbilical-Center, Co-Place, drived from Metzli, "The Center of the Moon"; A mountain peak that resembles the umbilical

MICTLAN: Mic-Micqui-Death; Tlan-Place; "Place where the Spirits Repose"; Topock Maze near Needles, California

MIXCOATL: Mix-Cloud, Coatl-Snake;

"Cloud of Snakes"; The Milky Way; The Riverside Mountains

MIXCOATCUAUHTLI: Mix-Cloud, Coatl-Snake, Cuauhtli-Eagle; Descending of the cosmos; Eagle image in the Big Maria Moutnains

MOCTEZUMA: The 9th Tlatoani of the Mexica, killed by Cortes in 1519

NAHUA: Na-Beginning, Hua-Possesor; the original Uto-Aztcan nations that migrated from the Colorado River

NAHUALLI: your spiritual anima/animus counterpart

NAHUATL: The Nahua Language

NAHUATLACA: Nahuatl speaker

NAHUI-OLLIN: Nahui-Four, Ollin-Movement; "The Four Movements/Directions"

NELITZTLI: To Seek the Roots of the Truth

NICARAGUA: Nica-Nican-Here, Aragua-Nahua; "Up to here came the Nahua"

OCELOTL: Jaguar, the Nahualli of Omecihuatl; Represents the Female

OMECIHUATL: Ome-Two (Spiritual & Physical), Cihuatl-Female Energy; Represents Mother Earth, in the cosmos Cassiopeia; one of the giant geoglyphs of the Blythe Giant Intaglios

OMETECUHTLI: Ome-two (Spiritual & Physical), Tecuhtli-Male Energy; Represents Orion the hunter in the cosmos; one of the giant geoglyphs of the Blythe Giant Intaglios

OMETEOTL: Ome-Two (Male & Female Spirits), Teotl-Energy; The Creator; One of the giant geoglyphs of the Blythe Giant Intaglios

OMEYOCAN: Ome-Two/Spiritual, Yo-Yolotl-Heart, Can-Place; "Place of the two Hearts" Metaphysical home of Ometeotl; 13th level of Knowledge; Cosmic Diamond of Infinity that overlaps the Palo Verde/Parker Valleys.

PILLI: Señor-Elder; Our Lord

QUETZALCOATL: Quetzal-Quetzalli-Precious Plumed, Coatl-Serpent-Twin; "The Plumed Serpent"; The principle image of the Creator represented by Venus, the Morning Star, Ehecatl-Wind and the Evening Star, Xolotl/Dog.

TAMOANCHAN: Ta-Tata-Grandfather-Cosmos, Moan-Descend-Merge, Chan-Chante-House-Earth; "Cosmos Descends to Earth" Decribed by the natives as "The Place where Sky meets Earth"; Granite Peak, mountain peak northwest of Blythe, looks like a pyramid at the end of the McCoy Valley.

TECPATL: Flint

TENOCHTITLAN: Te-Tetl-Rock, Noch-Nopal-Cactus, Ti-Merging, Tlan-Place; "Place where the Cactus grew from the Rock"; the island where Mexico City is located; the name was taken from the Big Maria Mountain by the Aztec

TEOCALLI: Teo-Teotl-Energy, Calli-House, "House of Energy; commonly called pyramids

TEOCULHUACAN: Teo-Energy, Cul-Colli-

Twisted, Hua-Possessor, Can-Place; Place of the Divine Tatas (grandfathers); a twisted mountain peak on the Big Maria Mountains

TEOMAMA: Teo-Teotl-Energy, Mama-Mother; the four energies, bundlekeepers shown in the Boturini Codex that took the knowledge from the Colorado River to all parts of the world

TEOTIHUACAN: Teo-Teotl-Energy, Tihua-Coming, Can-Place; "Place of the coming of the Energies"; the pyraminds north of Mexico City; relates to the coming of the enrgies on August 13

TEZCATLIPOCA: Tez-Tezcatl-Mirror, Ca-Calli-House-Mother Earth, Tli-Tlilli-Black, Poca-Smoke-Refelction; "The Black House of the Mirrored Reflection"; your memory/conscience; the southern peak of the Big Maria Mountains

TIANGUIS: The marketplace of the Mexica culture; the Pleiades in the cosmos, "The Seven Sisters Constellation"

TIZAPAN: Tiza-Chalk, Apan-by the water

TLACUILO: Painter and designer of Codices; "The Knowledge Keepers"

TLALOC: Female energy, duality of Huitzilopochtli, represents earth; associated with rain, water; the staff of Tlaloc represents lightning connecting the cosmos, humans and Mother Earth; fertility and reproduction; its nahualli is the frog whose imge is one of the peaks of Spirit Mountain and its geoglyph is the Bouse Fisherman

TLALOCAN: Place of Tlaloc, the Terrestial Paradise where the spirits repose, located near the Colorado River at Spirit Mountain north of Laughlin, Nv

TLAMANTINI: Teacher

TLALTECUHTLI: Tlal- Tlalli-Earth, Tecutli-Male; Center face of the Aztec Sunstone calendar; Mountain image on the south side of the Big Maria Mountains.

TLATOANI: Tlatoa-Word, Ani-Speaks; "He who speaks the Word"; Spokesperson of the Tlatocan/Mexica Senate

TLOQUE-NAHUAQUE- Supreme law, the close and together, the energy of everything symbolized by the fingers on the hand, different sizes and shapes but all coming together in the palm of the hand, base on the concept of "Among All, We Do All for the Benefit of All"

TONALLATLATZALIZTLI: The calm of the first sunrise of the first Sun during the spring equinox on the Moon Mountain Twin Peaks

TONANTZIN: To-Tonali-Sun/Energy, Na-Nana-Mother Earth, Tzin-Respect-Veneration; "Our Venerated Mother"; image in the Dome Rock Moutnain east of the Palo Verde Valley on December 21, the peak image shadows from 3:15 to 3:45 pm; the southern point of the Omeyocan Diamond

TONATIUH: To-Sun, Na-Energy, Tiuh-Path; The first sun ray breaking dawn during the equinoxes at the Moon Mountains. The sun shines on the pyramid image peak of Tonatiuhichan, house of the sun, on the ridge of the Big Maria Mountains

UAHUNCHE Symbol of protection of the Mayan culture; a strategy used by the traditionalist indigenous to preserve their culture. When the Euroopean Priest would preach, they would "See but not observe, hear but not listen", the reason the Mexica/Mayan traditional culture survived the 500 years of European rule (Hunbatz Men)

UTO-AZTECAN: Largest lingustic family in the western hemisphere; they extended from Montana in the north dow through the upper and lower Colorado River Basin to the San Clemente Islands, east to Texas and south to Nicaragua; millions of descendents of these families still speak Nahuatl

XICANO(A): One who defends his culture and seeks his indigenous roots

XICOMOZTOC: Xicom-Xicome-Seven, Oztoc-Cave; the woman's vulva/womb; the seven organs for the semen to pass to create the fetus

XOCHITLPILLI: Xochitl-Flower, Pilli-Lord; Image on the Big Maria Mountains represents the navel to the cosmos

XOLOTL: Dog; Evening Star; Duality of Ehecatl (morning star)

YEITILIZTLI: The three energies

Bibliography

Acamapixtli Garcia, J. M *Gobiernantes de Anahuac,* Artes y Reproduccion, S.A., Mexico, 1989

Aconcagua, Ediciones, *Ichcateopan, La Tumba de Cuauhtemoc*, Mexico 1973

Acosta, Joseph de, *Historia Natural y Moral de las Indias*, Fondo de Cultura Economica Mexico, 1940

Acuña, Rodolfo "Rudy", *Anything but Mexican: Chicanos in Comtemporary Los Angeles*, 2000;
Occupied American: A Chicano Struggle towards Liberation, 1972

Alemán Velasco Miguel, *La Isla de los Perros*, Editorial Diana, México, 1980

Alcalá, Manuel, *Hernán Cortes, Cartas de Relación*, Editorial Porrúa, 1985

Almada, Francisco R, *Diccionario de Historia Geografía y Biografía Sonorenses,* Instituto Sonorense de Cultura, México, 1990

Alvarado Tezozomoc, Hernando, *Crónica Mexicana*, Editorial Leyenda S.A, México, 1944
Crónica Mexicayotl, Imprenta Universitaria, México, 1949

Anders, Ferdinand, Et al, *Introducción y Explicación del Códice Borbónico*, Fondo de Cultura Económica México 1991, Fondo de Cultura Económica, 1992

Anzures, Maria *Coyolxuahqui Nuestra Madre Cósmica*, Consejo Nacional de la Cultura Náhuatl, 1991

Barlow, H. Roberto, *Los Mexicas y La Triple Alianza*, Obras del Instituto Nacional de Antropología e Historia (Traducción, Jesús Monjaras Ruiz), 1990

Barnes, Will C. Arizona Place Names, University of Arizona, 1960

Basurto, Carmen, G. *México y sus Símbolos*, Editorial Avante, S.A. 1983

Berkowitz, Franz Rayón, *La Antigua Nacameri, Sonora Mágica y Desconocida*, Hermosillo, Sonora México, 1990

Bernal, Ignacio, *Tres Científicos Mexicanos*, Secretaria de Educación Publica, 1974;
Tenochtitlan en un Isla, Secretaria de Educación Pública, 1984

Bierhorst, John *Codex Chimalpopoca, The Text in Nahuatl*, U. A. Press, 1992
History and Mythology of the Aztecs, Codex Chimalpopoca, U. A. Press, 1992

Bonilla, Manuel *De Atlatlan a México, Peregrinación de los Nahuas*, Sinaloa, Mexico, 1942

Broda, Johanna *The Great Temple of Tenochtitlan*, University of California Press

Buelna, Eustaquio, *Geográficos Indígenas de Sinaloa, Peregrinación de los Aztecas*, Del Agua Impresiones, 1887

Burland, C.A. *Montezuma Lord of the Aztec*, G.P. Putman and Sons, 1975

Byland, Bruce E. *Introduction and Commentary of the Codex Borgia*, Dover

Publication, 1993

Caine, Ralph L., *Historic Aztlán and The Laguna de Oro*, Los Angeles, 1962

Calvo Berber, Laureano, *Nociones de Historia de Sonora*, Manuel Porrúa, S.A., México, 1958

Capillio, Cuautli, Héctor, La Nación Mexicana, Fernández Editores, S.A. 1965

Carrasco, David, *Moctezuma's Mexico Visons of the Aztec World*, University Press of Colorado, 2003;
Quetzalcoatl and the Irony of Empire, University Press of Colorado, 2000

Caso, Alfonso, *The Aztec People of the Sun*, University of Oklahoma, 1958

Castillo, Cristobal de., *Historia de la Venida de los Mexicanos y otros Pueblos e Historia de la Conquista*, INAH, 1991

Chavero, D. Alfredo, *Los Aztecas o Mexicas, Fundacion de México/Tenochtitlan*, Jorge Porrúa, S.A. 1984
Historia Antigua y de la Conquista, México a Través de los Siglos, Editorial Cumbre, S.A. México, 1976

Chimalpain, Francisco de San Anton Muñon. *Relaciones Originales de Chalco Amaquemecan*, Traducción de S. Rendon FCE, México, 1965

Clavijero, Francisco Javier, *Historia Antigua de México*, Editorial Porrúa S.A. 1982

Codex Aubin, Manuscrito Azteca de la Biblioteca real de Berlin Anales en Mexicano y Geroglificos desde la salida de las tribus de Aztlán, Sr Bernardino de Jesús Quiroz,

Editorial Innovacion, S.A. México

Codex, Azcatitlan, Journal de la Sociedades, Americanistas de Paris, 1949

Codex Bodley, Maarten Jansen, The Boldeian Library, 2005

Codex Borgia, Los Templos del Cielo y de la Oscuridad, Ferdinand Anders Fondo de Cultura Económica 1993

Codex Borbonico, El Libro del Ciuacoatl, Ferdinand Anders, Fondo de Cultura Económica, 1991

Codex Boturini, Su Caminar de los Aztecas Lic Lucio Carpanta Baron, Fundacion Cultura

Codex Chimalpahin, Volume 1, Arthur J.O. Anderson, University of Oklahoma Press, 1997

Codex Chimalpahin, Volume 2, Arthur J.O. Anderson, University of Oklahoma Press, 1997

Codex Chimalapopoca, Anales de Cuauhtitlan y Leyenda de los Soles Primero, Feliciano Velazquez, Imprenta Universitaria México, 1945

Codex en Cruz, Charles E. Dibble, México 1942

Codex De Solei

Codex El Lienzo de Tlaxcalla, Alfredo Calvero, Editorial Cosmos, 1979

Codex Fejervary-Mayer, El Libro de Tezcatlipoca, Señor del Tiempo, Ferdinand Anders, Fondo de Cultura Económica, 1994

Codex Florentine, Historial General de Las Cosa Nueva España, Fr. Bernardino de Sahagun

Codex Florentine, Arthur J. O. Anderson, School of American Research, Charles E. Dibble, University of Utah

Codex Laud, Carlos Martínez Marín, Instituto Nacional de Antropología e Historia México, 1961

Codex Magaliabecchi, An Anonymous Hispano-Mexican Manuscript preserved at the Bibliotheca Nazionale-Centrale, Florence, Italy, Zelia Nuttal, University of California, Berkeley, 1903

Codex Mapa de Siguenza, Museo Nacional de Antropología, Biblioteca Central de INAH, 1982

Codex Nuttall, A Picture Manuscript from Ancient Mexico, Zelia Nuttall, Dover Publications, 1975

Codex Ramirez, Relación del origen de los indios que habitan en la Nueva España según sus historias. Colección de Documentos Conmemorativos de DCL Aniversario de la Fundacion de Tenochtitlan México, 1975

Codex Siguenza, Los Mexica parten de Culhuacan, 1980

Codex Telleriano-Remensis, Ritual, Divination and History in a Pictorial Aztec Manuscript, Eloise Quiñones Keber, University of Texas Press, 1995

Codex Vaticano A, Religión, Costumbres e Historia de los Antiguos Méxicanos, Ferdinand Anders Fondo de Cultura Económica, 1996

Codex Vindobonensis, Origen e Historia de los Reyes Mixtecos, Ferdinand Anders, Fondo de Cultura Económica, 1992

Codex Xolotl, Charles E. Dibble, Universidad Nacional Autónoma de México

Coe, Michael, *México* Praeger Publishers, 1966

Colin, Mario, *Nombres Geográficos Indígenas del Estado de México*, Biblioteca Enciclopedia de Estado de México, 1966

Cook, Fred S. History of Parker and Area, Parker, Az, 1985

Current, Richard N., et at, American History: A Survey

Davies, Nigel, *Los Antiguos Reinos de México*, Fondo de Cultura Económica, 1995 The Toltecs until the Fall of Tulla, University of Arizona Press

Day, Jane, S, *Aztec*, Denver Museum of Natural History, Rivehart Publishers, 1992

Dellenbaugh, Federick S. *The Romance of the Colorado River*, Dover Publications, 1998

Dominguez Hidalgo, Antonio, *De Hombres y Doses*, El Colegio de Michoacan

Duran, Diego, *The History of the Indians of New Spain,* (Traducion al Ingles: Doris Heyden), University of Oklahoma Press, 1994

Emmerich, Andre, Art before Columbus, Simon and Schuster, 1963

Emory, William Major, United States and Mexican Boundary Border Commission Report 1853-1854

Fabila, Alfonso, *La Tribus Yaquis de Sonora* México, 1965

Forbes, Jack D. *Only Approved Indians*, University of Oklahoma Press, 1994
Aztecas del Norte, The Chicanos of Aztlan, Fawcett Premiere Book, 1973
Native American of California and Nevada, Nature Graph Publisher, 1969
Warrior of the Colorado River, University of Oklahoma Press,

Fradkin, Philli L, *A River No More the Colorado River and the West*, UA Press, 1981

Franch, José, Alcina, Codice Mexicanos, Fundacion MAPERE America

Fulson, Charles Scrivner, *Mojave People*, Naylor Comp, San Antonio Tx, 1970

Galindo Trejo, Jesus, Arqueoastronomía, Editorial Equipo Csirius S.A, 1994

Gallo, Edwardo, *Cuauhtemoc, Ultimo Emperador de Mexico*, Editorial Innovación, S.A. 1980

Galving, John, *Fray Francisco Garces, A Record of Travel in Arizona and California 1775, 1776*, Howell Books

García Contreras, Guillermo, Los Códices Mayas, Secretaria de Educación Publica, 1975

García Quintana, Josefina, Cuauhtémoc en el Siglo XIX, UNAM, 1977

Garibay, K Angel Maria, *Historia de la Literatura Nahuatl, Primera y Segunda Parte*, Editorial, Porrúa, 1953
Llave de Nahuatl, Editorial Porrúa, 1961

Teogonía e Historia de los Mexicanos, Tres Opúsculos de Siglo XVI, Editorial Porrúa,

Gomora, A (Xokonochtletl) Juicio a España, Testigo Aztekas, Editorial Tlamatini, 1988

Gonzalez Obregon, Luis, *Cuauhtémoc*, Jorge Porrúa, S.A. 1984

Gordon, Willey R, *Trincheras Culture: An Introduction to American Archaeology*, 1966

Grey, Herman, *Tales from the Mohaves*, University of Oklahoma, 1970

Gruzinski, Sege, *The Aztecs, Rise and Fall of an Empire*

Gutiérrez, Tibon, *Historia del nombre y de la fundación de México*, 1993

Gutiérrez Solana, Nelly, Codices de México, Panorama Editorial, S.A., 1990

Hassler, Peter, *Human Sacrifice Among Aztecs*, P. Lang Publishers, Berlin, Germany, 1992

Haenszel M. Arda, *The Topock Maze: Commercial or Aboriginal*, San Bernardino County Museum

Heyden, Doris, México *Origen de un símbolo Mito y simbolismo en la Fundacion de México/Tenochtitlan*, Colección Distrito Federal, 1988
México Orígenes de un Símbolo, INAH, México, 1998

Hinton, Leann, et.al, *History of the Colorado River Reservation*, CRIT, 1947

Infante Diaz, Fernando, *La Estela de los Soles Calendario Azteca*, Panorama Editorial

S.A. 1999

Instituto de Investigaciones, Historia del Estado de Baja California, II Simposio de Historia, marzo, 21, 1986

Kirchhoff, Paul, et al, *Historia Tolteca-Chichimeca, Consejo Nacional para la Cultura y las Artes*, México, 1992

Kroeber, A.I, *Handbook of the Indian of California*, Dover Publications, 1976
Seven Mohave Myths, A Mohave War, Reminiscence 1854-1880, Dover Publications, 1973

Kroeber, B Clifton, et. Al., *Massacre on the Gila*, University of Arizona, 1992

Laird, Carol Beth, *The Chemehuevis*, Malki Museum, Banning, Ca, 1976

Landa, Diego de, Relación de las Cosa de Yucatán, Consejo Nacional para la Cultura y las Artes, 1994

Langston, de Salazar, Manuelita, San Ignacio Rio Muerto, Municipio de Guaymas,

López-Austin, Alfredo, Tamoanchan y Tlalocan, Fondo de Cultura

López Navarro Raúl, *El Numero 13 en vida de los Aztecas*, Proculmex, S.A. 1994
El Peregrinar de los Aztecas, Costa-AMIC Editores, S.A, 1996

López Velarde, Ramon, El Códice de Cuauhtémoc, UNAM, 1980

Lowell Bean, John, et al. Cahuilla Indians of California, Malki Museum Press, 1967

Macazaga, Ordeno Cesar, *Nombres Geográficos de México*, Editorial Renovación, S.A. 1980

Magaloni Duarte, Ignacio, *Educadores del Mundo, 1971*, Costa AMIC Editores, S.A.1996

Manchip White, Jon, Hernán Cortes, Ediciones Grijalbo, S.A., 1974

Martínez, Pablo, *Historias del Estado de Baja California*, Instituto de Investigaciones, Mexicali, B.C., 1986

Martínez Pérez, Héctor, *Cuauhtémoc, Hijo del Sur*, Taxco Guerrero, 1962
Cuauhtémoc, Vida y Muerte de Una Cultura, Gobierno de Estado de Campeche, 1993
Masterworks of Mexican Art, Los Angeles County Museum of Art, 1963-1964

Matos Moctezuma, Eduardo, *The Great Temple,* INAH, 1992

Men, Hunbatz, Los Calendarios Astronómicos Maya y Hunab Ku, Ediciones Horizonte, 1983
Secrets of Mayan Science/Religion, Gear Company, Santa Fe, New Mexico, 1990

Meza Gutiérrez, Arturo, *Reminiscencias de Malinalco*, Instituto Mexiquense de Cultura, 1995

Miller Dean, Ronald, et. Al., *The Chemehuevi Indians of Southern California*, Malki Museum, Banning, Ca 1967

Miller, Mary, et. al., An Illustrated Dictionary of the Gods and Symbols of Ancient Mexico and the Maya, Thames and Hudson, Publisher, 1997

Millon, Rene, *Teotihuacan*, University of

Texas, 1993
The Teotihuacan Map, University of Texas, 1973

Molina, Felipe S. et. al., A concise Yoeme and English Dictionary, Tucson Unified School District, Bilingual Education and Hispanic Studies Department, 1993

Molina Molina, Flavio, et. al., *Nombres Indígenas de Sonora y su Traducción al español*, Hermosillo, Sonora, 1972
Relacion de Saguaripa, 1778, Hermosillo, Sonora, 1974

Moreno Toscano, Alejandra, *Hallazgos de Ichcateopan*, 1949-1951, UNAM, 1980

Moreno, Marco Antonio, *Historia de la Astronomía en México*, S.E.P., 1986

Motolinía, Toribio, *Historia de la Indias de la Nueva España*, Editorial Porrúa, 1990

Munro, Pamela, et. al., A Mojave Dictionary, UCLA Linguistics Dept, 1992

Muñon, Don Francisco de San Antón, *Relaciones Originales de Chalco Amaquemecan*, Fondo de Cultura Económía
The Native America, An Illustrated History, Turner Publishing, Inc. 1983

Olivera de Bonfil, Alicia, *La Tradición Oral Sobre Cuauhtémoc*, UNAM, 1980

Nava, Julian, *My Mexican-American Journey*

Nicholson, Irene, *Mexican and Central American Mythology*, The Hamlyn Publishing Group Limited, 1975

Nowotny, Karl Anton, *Tlacuilolli*, University of Oklahoma Press, 2005

Ordoño, Cesar Macazaga, Nombres Geográficos de México, Editorial Cosmos, 1979 México DFMX

Orozco y Berra, Manuel, Historial de la Ciudad de México, Desde su Fundacion hasta 1854, Secretaria de Educación Pública, 1973

Ortiz, de Zarate, Gonzalo, *Petroglificos de Sinaloa*, Fomento Cultural Banamex, A.C., México, 1976

Pérez, R. Esther, *Orgullo de Aztlan, Una Reseña Historia Mexicana,* Guadalajara, Jalisco, 1972

Portillo, León Miguel, *El Mito del Nacimiento de Huitzilopochtli, Códice Florentino*
Aztec Thought and Culture, University of Oklahoma Press, 1982
Los Antiguos Mexicanos, Fondo de Cultura Económica, 1965
Quince Poetas de Mundo Nahuatl, Editorial Diana, 1994

Reyes García, Luis, Documentos Manuscritos y Pictóricos de Ichcateopan, Guerrero, UNAM, 1979

Robledo, Cecilio A. Diccionario Nahuatl

Rodríguez, Salvador, Cuauhtémoc, Ixcateopan, Guerrero, mayo 18, 1987

Romero Quiroz, Javier, México, "En el Centro de la Luna", Gobierno del Estado de México
Nacimiento de Huitzilopochtli: Solsticio de Invierno en Malinalco, Instituto Mexicanense de Cultura, 1990

Romerovargas Yturbide, Ignacio, Los

Gobiernos Socialistas de Anáhuac, Romervargas, Editor, S.A., 1978

Motecuhzoma Xocoyotzin o Moctezuma el Magnífico y La Invasión de Anáhuac, Romervargas y Blasco Editores, S.A. III Tomos Primera Edición, 1957

Organización Política de los Pueblos de Anáhuac, Romerovargas y Blasco Editores, S.A. Primera Edición, 1964

Rurner, R. Paul, The Highland Chontal, Secretaria de Educación, Publicada, 1973

Saxton, Dean, Dictionary Papago/Pima-English, U.A. Press, 1983

Seguy, Rose Marie, Aztlan: Terre des Azteque; Images d'un Nouveao Monde, Bibliotheque Nationale Paris, 1976

Seiler Hans, Jakob, et. al., Cahuilla Dictionary, Malki Museum Press, Banning CA, 1979

Setzler, Grady, Another Wilderness Conquered, Palo Verde Times, Segunda Edicion, 1972

Scofield, Bruce, Signs of Time: An introduction to Mesoamerican Astrology, One Reed Publications, 1994

Shaw, Anna Moore, Pima Indian Legends, U.A. Press

Sherman, James, et. al., Ghost Towns of Arizona

Simeon, Remi, Diccionario de la Lengua Nahuatl Mexicana, Siglo Veintiuno, S.A. 1981

Smith A., Gerald. The Mojaves, San Bernardino County Museum, 1977

Sobarzo, Horacio. Vocabulario Sonorense, Fomento y Cultura del Gobierno de Sonora, 1991

Soutelle, Jacques. *Daily Life of the Aztecs*, Stanford University Press, 1970; El Universo de los Aztecas, 1991

Spicer N. Edward. Cycles of Conquest, University of Arizona Press, 1992

Spier, Leslie. Yuman Tribes of the Gila River, Dover Publications, 1978

Sten, Maria. Codices of México, Panorama Editorial, México, 1990

Teja Zabre, Alfonso, Breve Historia de México

Tezozomoc, Hernando A. Crónica Mexicayotl, Editorial Leyenda, S.A. 1944

Torquemada, Fray Juan de. Monarquía indiana Volumen 1, 2, 3. Universidad Nacional Autónoma de México Instituto de Investigaciones Históricas México, 1975

Toscano, Salvador. Cuauhtémoc, Fondo de Cultura Económica, 1975

Vaillant G., C. Aztecs of Mexico, Pelican Book, 1966

Velázquez Primo, Feliciano. Códices Chimalpopoca, imprenta Universitaria México, 1945

Verrill Hyatt, A., et.al. America's Ancient Civilization, J.P. Putnam Sons, 1953

Von Humboldt, Alexander. Political Essay on the Kingdom of New Spain, Alfred Knopf, 1972

Wagoner Jay, J. Arizona Territory, 1863-1912, A Political History, University of Arizona Press, 1980

Waters, Frank. The Colorado, Shallow Press 1984 Magazine and Other Sources Consulted: American Archaeology and Ethnology, Vol. II, No. 4, February 10, 1915

Magazines and Other Sources Consulted:

American Archaeology and Ethnology, Vol II No 4, February 10, 1915

Apodaca, Paul. First Voices: Indigenous Music of Southern California, Bowers Museum Pamphlet

Avalos, Enrique de Lira. Zona Arqueológica de Piedra Verde, El Sol de Durango, agosto 30 de 1991

Barrie, Steven. Inland Catholic Newspaper, June 1996

Bassett, Carol Ann. Mystery of the Desert Giants, American West Magazine, March/April 1986

Boynton, Margaret. Chief Francisco Patencio: Stories and Legends of the Palm Springs Indians, Times Mirror Press, 1943

Brumgardt, John R. Historical Portrait of Riverside County, (Ed.), Riverside County Historical Commission, 1977

Castetter, Edward, et.al, Yuma Indian Agriculture Ce-Acatl: Revista de la Cultura de Anahuac # 6, noviembre, 1991, Mexico D. F.

Champe, Waters Flavia.The Matachines Dance of the Upper Rio Grande: History, Music, and Choreography, University of Nebraska Press, 1983

Cibola National Wildlife, Refuge, U.S. Department of Interior, Pamphlet

Dekens, Camile. Riverman, Desertman, Press Enterprise

Devereaux, George. Mojave Cheiftaninship in Action Northern Arizona Society and Art Plateau Vol. 23, No. 3, 1951

Figueroa, Alfredo A. La Ira del Águila, Documentary Script 1973
¡Salven Nuestros Sitios Antiguos Sagrados...! Southwest Network for Environmental & Economic Justice 2005

González Soto, Guillermo Jaime. Ingeniería Humana, La Ciencia de Los Mayas, panfleto

Guzmán, Eulalia. Donde Estuvo el Aztlan de los Mexicas. Órgano de la Sociedad de Investigaciones. Historia de México, Boletín Cuatrimestral, nov., 1966, abril, 1967

Johnson, Boma. Earth Figures of the Lower Colorado and Gila Rivers Desert, Arizona Archaeological Society,

Johnston, Francis J. & Patricia. An Indian Trail complex of the Central Colorado Desert California, Archeology Journal, April 1, 1957

Marshall C. George. Giant Effigies of the Southwest, National Geographic Magazine,

September 1952

Morton, Paul K. California Division of Mines: Geology and Mineral Resources of Imperial County, 1977

Ortiz, Ruben, et.al. Frontier Land (Documentary), 1995 Publication in American Archaeology and Ethnology, Vol. II, No. 4, February 10, 1915

Sherer, M. Lorraine. The Clan System of the Mojave Indians, So Ca Quarterly XLVII, March 1965

Swerdlow L. Joel. Human Culture, National Geographic Magazine, January 1998 Newspaper, Beautyway, The Californian Historical Journal,

Thomas, Cyrus, Indian Languages of Mexico and Central America, Smithsonian Institution, Bureau of American Ethnology, Bulletin 1911

Utah Postcard, Rock State Park Newspaper, Beautyway

Warren Von Till, Elizabeth. Cultural Resources of the California Desert, Historical Trails and 1Vagon Road, 1776- 1980, Bureau of Land Management, 1981

Willey R. Gordon. Trincheras Culture; An Introduction to American Archaeology, 1966

Woodward, Arthur. Gigantic Intaglio Pictographs in the Californian Desert, The Illustrated London News, September 10, 1932

McDonald, Observatorio. Ascienden las Pléyades, noviembre 14 de 2003, página de Internet de la Universidad de Texas

www.ingramcontent.com/pod-product-compliance
Lightning Source LLC
Chambersburg PA
CBHW060316240426
43661CB00059B/2782